Pay
Dirt

Pay Dirt

HOW TO MAKE $10,000 A YEAR FROM YOUR BACKYARD GARDEN

John Tullock

Aadamsmedia

Avon, Massachusetts

Published by
Adams Media, a division of F+W Media, Inc.
57 Littlefield Street, Avon, MA 02322. U.S.A.
www.adamsmedia.com

ISBN 10: 1-60550-349-5
ISBN 13: 978-1-60550-349-3

Printed in the United States of America.

10 9 8 7 6 5 4 3 2 1

Library of Congress Cataloging-in-Publication Data
is available from the publisher.

This publication is designed to provide accurate and authoritative information with regard to the subject matter covered. It is sold with the understanding that the publisher is not engaged in rendering legal, accounting, or other professional advice. If legal advice or other expert assistance is required, the services of a competent professional person should be sought.

—From a *Declaration of Principles* jointly adopted by a Committee of the American Bar Association and a Committee of Publishers and Associations

Many of the designations used by manufacturers and sellers to distinguish their product are claimed as trademarks. Where those designations appear in this book and Adams Media was aware of a trademark claim, the designations have been printed with initial capital letters.

This book is available at quantity discounts for bulk purchases.
For information, please call 1-800-289-0963.

Acknowledgments

No book is solely the work of its author, and this one is no exception. Many people have freely given me advice over the years, and their influence has shaped the notions I have set down here. I am indebted to the scores of farmers' market vendors who took time to chat with me, however briefly, about their aspirations. I don't know their names, but to them must go my thanks for all their insights regarding the ins and outs of making money farming vegetables and flowers, whether on a micro or macro scale. Special thanks must go to Bob Due, Lori McAlister, Teresa Myrick, Sheri Palko, and Ann Stuck for their enthusiasm for this project.

I am fortunate to live in an area with numerous excellent nurseries and garden centers run by dedicated and independent-minded proprietors. In particular, Beth Cox, Monte Stanley, Mike Stansberry, and Greg and Diane Ellenburg have always made my involvement in the plant business a pleasure.

My interest in gardening was sparked by my grandparents, Faye and Clarence Boswell, who passed away in 1966 and 1976, respectively. In the intervening decades, the simple arts they taught me have grown ever more precious in a world where living in harmony with nature has become an exception, rather than the rule.

Despite a lifelong involvement with growing things, I would never have become a market gardener had it not been for the unflagging support and tireless labor of my partner of thirty-five years, Jerry Yarnell. Without his encouragement, this book would never have been started, much less completed. For this, I am deeply grateful.

Thanks to my best pal, Graham Byars, for his helpful comments, suggestions, and abundant (though always constructive) criticisms. One could not ask for a better gardening buddy. Thanks also to friends Terry Richman and Scott Morrell, growers of beautiful blooms.

Finally, many thanks to my agent, Grace Freedson. This volume is the seventh title we have collaborated on. Words are inadequate to express my gratitude for the dedication and hard work she puts into every book.

Sources

The Appendix contains many resources for the would-be suburban farmer. All of the references cited in that chapter were consulted for information contained in the far-ranging discussions throughout the book. Some sources were not included in the Appendix, because of their purely historical value as background information that, hopefully, helps to illuminate the concepts addressed.

The newspaper article mentioned in Chapter 1 can be found at *http://online.wsj.com/article/SB120903237167241285 .html?mod=WSJBlog*.

The short biography of Rachel Carson in Chapter 6 is based on information from *www.rachelcarson.org* authored by Linda Lear, the biography posted by the U.S. Fish and Wildlife Service at *www.fws .gov/northeast/rachelcarson/carsonbio.html*, and the Wikipedia entry *http://en.wikipedia.org/wiki/Rachel_Carson*.

The brief discussion in Chapter 6 of the work of Justus von Liebig draws upon the Wikipedia entry *http://en.wikipedia.org/wiki/ Justus_von_Liebig* and one from the Encyclopedia Britannica posted at *www.1902encyclopedia.com/L/LIE/justus-liebig.html*.

Important dates in the history of *Bacillus thuringiensis* (Bt) were obtained from *www.bt.ucsd.edu/bt_history.html*.

All these web postings were confirmed as of December 20, 2008.

Despite all the expert advice, errors and omissions have no doubt crept into the discussions that follow. The blame for those mistakes rests entirely on my shoulders.

contents

chapter one

Money *Does* Grow on Trees

Could you use an extra $10,000 next year? Do you live in a house with some land around it? If the answer to both questions is "Yes!" you should consider joining the burgeoning "suburban microfarm" movement. Like so much else associated with food, soil, and life, the movement has its roots, if you will pardon the pun, in California. But as a *Wall Street Journal* article—highlighting a successful suburban farm in Colorado—makes clear, this new type of agriculture is not just for California any more.

Gardeners across the United States are harvesting big bucks from remarkably tiny plots. When I was a suburban farmer in Knoxville, Tennessee (population about 250,000), my partner and I grew nursery stock on a 60-foot by 200-foot lot, and we still had plenty of room for a kitchen garden. In one season, we sold over $14,000 worth of plants.

The Time Is "Ripe"

Turning a green thumb into greenbacks takes ingenuity and planning, but seldom has there been a better time to try your hand at such a project than today. Backyard farming has increased in popularity as suburban dwellers seek both extra cash and personal satisfaction by growing and selling their own produce. Clearly, in this time of economic hardships, rising food prices, and concerns about the environment, the notion of turning their backyard into a microfarm appeals to many people.

Suburban farming is not merely viable, it is sufficiently successful to be a rapidly spreading phenomenon, but as with other businesses, the competition is healthy. The niches available are numerous, and the demand for many products is continuous and unchanging. Even in an economic downturn, everyone has to eat. People often cut corners elsewhere in the household budget rather than sacrifice taste and quality in food. Many also know that local, sustainable production of foods, nursery stock, and cut flowers provides environmental benefits while saving consumers money.

Unfortunately, not everyone who tries this Earth-friendly approach to earning extra income succeeds. Expert gardeners may be lousy business operators, and vice versa. But if you have a penchant for growing things, average to above-average communication skills, and a head for business, and if you follow the advice presented in this book, you will find no problem in earning several thousand dollars in your first year. With your sales will come the satisfaction of earning money from the literal fruits of your labor, not to mention a bigger savings account, a bathroom or kitchen makeover, or just some financial help at the gas pump. That should spur you to even greater victories as a fledgling suburban microfarmer.

Make Money, Save the Planet

Besides being good for your pocketbook, suburban farming is good for your health and for the Earth. No one doubts the health benefits of exercise outdoors. The low-impact workout required for most garden activities is such that anyone in reasonable physical condition should be able to handle it.

Locally grown foods produced via organic or all-natural techniques not only taste better but they also retain more nutritional value, as compared to foods shipped from far away. Other types of products, from nursery stock to cut flowers, are cheaper for consumers when locally produced, because transportation is a negligible portion of their cost. As well, they use less energy, particularly fossil fuels, because of their lower transportation and storage costs. Furthermore, applying sustainable practices to the cultivation of these products helps reduce the demand for pesticides and chemical fertilizer. All these factors reduce the amount of fuel consumed and greenhouse gases released. Thus, when you join the suburban farmer movement, you're contributing to both healthy eating and sustainable living throughout your community.

Take the Five Steps to Profits

There are five basic steps to becoming a suburban farmer. Briefly, they are:

1. Find your market.
2. Find your product.
3. Evaluate your assets.
4. Create a business plan.
5. Execute!

Above all, locate your market(s) first. The biggest challenge facing any small business start-up is reaching consumers who are ready to buy. You can spend a fortune and waste huge amounts of time if you're a voice crying in the wilderness. Start by determining who might want to buy locally grown farm products and how you can bring your business to their attention.

- Do you have a local farmers' market or cooperative?
- Does it do plenty of business?
- Should you join?

Questions like these should be addressed first, because you must find the market, or more likely a combination of markets, that will give you the sales volume you need to make a profit.

Choosing a product line is step two. To people who are already gardeners, the choice of product may seem obvious. You grow what you love most or are most skillful at growing. Unfortunately, the consumers in your area may not want to buy those things, so you must choose products carefully. Nothing is more disheartening than sitting in your stall at the farmers' market, an array of botanical rarities in front of you, watching the neighboring vendor sell $1,000 worth of plants one can find at any big box retailer. Choosing your product wisely involves matching your resources with the markets you discovered in step one.

Once you have developed some ideas about where you can find sales and what you might be able to sell, it is time to evaluate the resources you can bring to the table.

Growing space is obviously the most important limitation on your money-making prospects, but your time is essential, too, and many of us just have no time to spare. You must be brutally honest with yourself about the commitment required. And of course there's the matter of budget. If you are looking for extra income already, it may be difficult to justify expenses for launching your farming venture. If after a straightforward assessment you remain convinced that a microfarm makes sense for your situation, proceed to the next step, creating a business plan.

Writing up a formal plan for a microfarm may seem like a waste of time, but in reality it is vital. Perhaps most importantly, a business plan will help you view the project as a business rather than a hobby. For those of us who already love plants and gardens, it is easy to justify foolish business decisions on the basis of our personal tastes in, and passions for, plants. Having a plan keeps you focused. It also permits you to quickly evaluate how the project is going financially.

Backyard production space

I have provided some examples that will help you put together a business plan tailored to the unique circumstances of your microfarming venture.

Finally, as with any worthwhile endeavor, you must execute the plan. Among gardeners stories abound regarding the ease of "planting on paper" while snow swirls around the eaves. That lush paper garden contrasts sharply with the stark realization of the amount of work involved when spring finally arrives. After you locate markets, fairly assess your capabilities and create a sound plan, I encourage you to grab a shovel and start digging in the "pay dirt."

chapter two

Sell What Sells

In a bygone era, small farmers planted a wide variety of crops, hauled them to town, and sold what they could. Today, agriculture experts exhort the aspiring farmer to identify the market before planting the first seed. This advice applies especially in the case of the suburban microfarmer. You will have little or no ability to compete in crops where sheer volume dictates production. Canneries, for example, require produce in truckloads, and their buyers could not be less interested in your perfect heirloom-variety tomatoes. Nevertheless, markets do exist for virtually anything you might produce, be it vegetables or nursery stock. Finding these markets locally should be your primary task as you develop your new backyard business.

Do You Mean "Market" or "the Market?"

Let's clarify what is meant by the term "market." In the narrowest sense, it refers to a specific location where sales occur, as in "farmers' market." In a broader sense, however, the "market" consists of all the people who might be customers for your products. "Marketing," therefore, is the act of offering your goods to potential buyers through all available means, not just across the counter. A more appropriate term for the across-the-counter effort is "selling." The important message here is that *marketing* involves a lot more than just trucking your goods to *the market*. Marketing includes:

- Coming up with business cards
- Running some advertising
- Launching a website
- Printing up some flyers to distribute from your truck

The better you are at marketing, the better you will do at the market. Sheri Palko produces sheep's milk cheeses on her Locust Grove Farm in the Tennessee Valley. "For the small producer of artisanal products," she says, "marketing involves taking careful aim at a moving target."

Markets Galore

Everyone needs to eat, and most vegetables can be raised from seed within three or four months. There are important reasons to consider vegetable production as a potential source of income. For one thing, many possible outlets exist for fresh produce, and several can usually be found in any community.

They include:

- Farmers' markets
- Flea and event markets
- Grocers

- Restaurants
- Community Supported Agriculture (CSA) arrangements

In addition to exploring these options, you may want to consider direct retail sales from your location, either via walk-in sales or pick-your-own. Mail-order selling offers yet another possibility.

Farmers' markets

Farmers' markets provide business locations where customers can purchase food, flowers, nursery stock, and other products directly from you the grower. Many variations on the basic farmers' market theme exist. You should visit all such venues in your area to fairly assess the available opportunities. In the ideal situation, the farmers' market permits sales only of products actually grown by the vendor. Most also permit growers to sell "value added" products, such as jams and pickles, provided the key raw materials, such as fruit or cucumbers, came from the vendor's garden. At the other end of the spectrum are public markets where anyone with something to sell can set up a table. You'll need to check the rules for any market you might contemplate joining.

Farmers' markets offer one of the best outlets for the suburban grower.

In my area, we have public markets operated by different entities. Downtown, in the county seat, lies Market Square, a traditional venue that once dominated commerce for farm products in the entire

PHOTO BY JOHN TULLOCK

Farmers' markets offer one of the best outlets for the suburban grower region. Now refurbished and surrounded by boutique restaurants and trendy shops, the Market Square Farmers' Market operates under the auspices of a nonprofit association made up of merchants and property owners in the Market Square area. The market, which is open two days a week, adheres to a producer-only policy, meaning only vendor-made products can be sold. Sales of craft items are permitted, along with fresh produce and related items such as honey, cut flowers, and nursery stock. A similar market is operated by the county department of parks, but it permits only farm produce and food products, not arts and crafts items. A third market is operated by an organization known as the Farmers Association for Retail Marketing (FARM). Also a producer-only market that allows no crafts, it is supported by the member farmers, and only they may sell at the twice-weekly markets.

One can argue the advisability of joining a market that permits craft items. On the one hand, crafts may bring in a larger crowd, but this also means more vendors compete for your customers' attention. The FARM-sponsored markets offer an interesting twist: in order to join the association you must pay a nominal fee to have your farm inspected, to assure that only products actually made by the vendors are on sale. Each of these market organizations receives some assistance from local sponsors and/or the state department of agriculture. The FARM program, for example, receives assistance, though no money, from the state. Tennessee has long leaned heavily on agriculture for much of its income, but in times past the bulk of the assistance went to producers of major crops, such as soybeans and tobacco. In recent years statewide efforts to encourage local food production, such as FARM, have begun to pay off not only for farmers but for consumers as well. Local restaurants have begun advertising their use of fresh, local ingredients, a sure sign that the public has grown aware of the benefits of eating close to home.

Go Local!

The trend toward local consumption bodes well for the would-be microfarmer, and Tennessee is not the only state to provide government support. A quick check of two states chosen at random,

Oklahoma and Virginia, turned up websites touting "Eat Local" programs sponsored by the agriculture departments in those states. Online directories of farmers' markets across the country are listed in the Appendix.

Rules and terms for participating in farmers' markets vary widely. In the case of my local FARM market, the costs include the one-time inspection fee, annual dues, and a percentage of each day's gross sales. These funds cover the administrative costs of the program, such as advertising in local media.

The FARM markets are well attended. As a frequent customer, I've often waited in line for the choicest items. I have observed that many vendors routinely sell out by the end of the day. Any market's success can be attributed to several factors. Access can be critical, for example. The downtown location mentioned above offers the widest array of products to tempt consumers, but its location presents a big challenge to the customer searching for convenient, low-cost parking. Not many consumers from the outlying suburbs find the time to patronize the market. Its customers mostly work downtown. On the other hand, the FARM market is located in a church parking lot on the busiest thoroughfare connecting the downtown area with its most densely populated suburbs. Thousands of cars pass by every day. Further, the immediate vicinity of the market is a residential area populated by upscale, educated consumers who recognize the value of local food and can afford to pay for it.

Get the Timing Right

Proper timing is also critical to the success of a farmers' market. Because the farmer has to be occupied most of the week with production, markets are usually held only on certain days and times. For the consumer, this largely means that the convenience of popping into the supermarket any time of day or night and finding fresh cilantro goes completely out the window. This means you must choose times that will offer the greatest possible convenience to customers without being too disruptive to essential farm work routines. The FARM market in our example is busiest on Friday afternoons, when it is open from 3:00 to 6:00 P.M. People frequently line up beginning at 2:30 or so. In canvassing others while standing in line, I have learned that many people plan weekend meals with family, as well as their weekend entertaining, around this Friday visit to the market. I suspect Friday markets do well in many locations for this reason alone.

All of this explains why visiting your local markets constitutes essential research. Of the three markets described, which one would you prefer to join? My choice as a seller is the one operated by farmers, at the location with the highest traffic, and open at the most convenient time for the majority of consumers in the area.

Flea and Event Markets

The classic version of this age-old type of venue for commerce is a weekend community gathering of buyers and sellers. In some areas, flea markets are operated as a commercial venture. You must pay a fee to gain access to selling space. Sales of anything and everything are allowed, and participation is open to any vendor with the rent money in hand. In my experience, flea markets may not be the best venue for farm products. They tend to be dominated by cheap merchandise and to be patronized by people looking for bargains rather than healthy food. Think "yard sale" on a grander scale. You might find customers for nursery stock, however, if you are considering this product area. Your best strategy is to visit the market several times to get an impression of the clientele it attracts as well as what's being sold.

Try Event Markets

Event markets are sales venues open only in connection with a special event. Craft fairs, holiday celebrations, and events sponsored by public institutions may all offer lucrative, if one-time-only, opportunities for the suburban microfarmer. While a food- or garden-themed event might be an obvious choice, I've spotted farm product vendors at events as unlikely as the opening of an art museum, so don't rule out any event with sales until you've thoroughly investigated it. Check local news listings for community events. Often the announcement will indicate whether vendors will be present.

Call or e-mail the contact given in the announcement and find out what is sold and by whom. If no contact information for the event is given in the ad, try calling the newspaper's advertising department to locate a contact. Sometimes sales at event markets are restricted. For example, businesses that have been benefactors of the sponsoring organization may be the only ones permitted to sell. Another possible obstacle you should anticipate is the popularity of such markets with vendors. You may have to get on a waiting list in order to get a spot at the more popular venues.

If you find an event market in your area that will accept you as a vendor and that offers a high likelihood of a profitable day or days of selling, by all means give it a try. Dedicated patrons of the event's sponsor can become good repeat customers for you. Even if your sales are slow, the event can advertise your presence in the community. Take advantage of every opportunity to do that essential marketing. If you plan to become a regular vendor at the farmers' market, for example, you might benefit from the exposure afforded by a springtime event sale.

Grocers Large and Small

Not until you become involved in the business of selling produce to a large grocery store will you appreciate the sheer volume of food that moves through your local neighborhood. For example, Grainger County, Tennessee, is famous for its high-quality tomatoes, and they are much in demand throughout the region. About twenty miles from where I live, I have friends who grow tomatoes on many acres. Their biggest customer is a single Kroger supermarket. This one store buys *four tons* of my friends' tomatoes each week. I repeat, four tons per week. This is in addition to piles of tomatoes imported from California and Mexico. Unless you fully comprehend their volume requirements—and can meet them—supermarkets may not offer the best outlet for your produce.

In addition to their need for massive amounts of fruits and vegetables, large grocery chains expect you to meet the strict quality and packaging standards adhered to by commercial vegetable brokers. Quality assurance standards are set by the USDA. Packaging standards developed by consensus over time, but have become strict rules with widespread use. Tomatoes, for example, come in forty-pound boxes, period. Variations from the expected are usually not acceptable to a large supermarket produce manager. This does not mean that they avoid new items, eschew gourmet quality, or disdain local purchasing, only that they expect these things also to conform to industry standards.

Small, independent grocers, though they have become a rare breed, offer you more opportunities than you are likely to find at the big chains. Since the owner can set policy on the spot, he or she may not be so persnickety about packaging, for example. And while quality will be your main selling point, it will not likely be necessary for each tomato to be the same diameter in order to be considered salable.

Restaurants

If you have one or more small gourmet restaurants in your area, you may be able to sell your products to them. Small restaurants use produce in relatively small quantities, yet must purchase from the same wholesale houses that supermarkets use. You may be lucky enough to find a chef who wants just the amount of zucchini blossoms or arugula you can produce, and is willing to pay a premium price for them.

If your area has several such restaurants, you have an opportunity to market different products to different chefs. Il Trattoria may want miniature basil leaves, while El Capitan has been looking for fresh poblano chilies, and The Happy Dragon will take all the baby bok choy you can grow. To locate the best potential restaurant customers in your area, start with the telephone directory. You can quickly eliminate many, such as delis and fast food chains, who are likely to want only commodity products. Your most suitable targets will be ethnic, vegetarian, and/or chef-owned establishments. For example, ethnic restaurants may be desperate for high-quality produce of certain preferred varieties. Restaurants catering to vegetarians are far more likely to be interested in local produce, heirloom varieties, and artisanal products than, say, a steak house chain. And the more upscale the restaurant, the more likely the chef will appreciate the special qualities of your finest produce offerings (and be willing to pay an appropriate price).

Make a list of all the possibilities you discover in the phone book. Next, call and ask if the chef is interested in local produce. If you can arrange a visit, you are halfway to a sale. Set up a time that is convenient for the chef. Be on time for the meeting, and take along samples of your offerings. Don't make the mistake of showing off only the most nearly perfect produce. Your samples should be a fair representation of what you have to offer. Chefs are notoriously picky and obsessive about their work, but a good chef can be a great customer, year in and year out.

Become a Foodie

The best way to learn what kinds of specialty produce might interest a restaurant is to become a foodie yourself. Check the restaurant reviews in your local media for insight. Look for restaurants touting their use of local products. This is becoming more and more common. Ask your friends to share their observations, and go eat at your top choices if you can afford it. Food magazines, such as *Saveur*, *Bon Appetit*, and *Cooks Illustrated*, will also help to clue you in on food trends. Regional magazines may have a section devoted to the local food scene. Watch the Food Network to see what the big-name chefs are cooking. Books presenting the cuisine at world-class restaurants, such as Chez Panisse in Berkeley, California, or Charlie Trotter's in Chicago, are available from libraries. Read the recipes for mention of specific vegetable and fruit varieties. Chances are, local chefs have read some of these books also and want to follow suit. You will quickly learn that chefs are highly competitive and the best ones pay close attention to food fashions. Focus your growing efforts on high-value specialty items not commonly available. For example, tiny new potatoes of an heirloom cultivar might be a good bet, but the chef at a trendy spot is not likely to be interested in buying standard baking potatoes from you. He can get them by the ton from any wholesaler.

If you find a chef who is enthusiastic about locally sourced produce, you may be able to arrange custom growing for the restaurant. Some chefs will actually sit down with you and go over a pile of seed catalogs, helping you decide what to grow the following season. If you can make such arrangements you will have a guaranteed market for your produce. Keep a couple of things in mind, however. Make sure the chef understands that, owing to the vagaries of weather and the nature of the plants themselves, crop failure is always a possibility. Also, make sure you give as much notice as possible if you cannot fill a prearranged order. Restaurant menus may be developed months in advance. Good chefs can compensate for a shortage, but only if you let them know what to expect. Failure to do so will most likely cost you their business. No one likes surprises of that kind. Not every city is blessed with restaurants that are eager to work with farmers, but the trend seems to be in that direction. Watch for your community's eateries to place more emphasis on local food as the cost of shipping rises.

Direct Selling

Taking your products directly to the public may be your only option if your area lacks existing market venues or if you cannot meet the requirements for participation in sponsored markets. Basically, direct selling means you load up your wares and haul them to a location where you'll be seen by passersby. This approach to marketing fresh produce may work when you have an abundant seasonal crop and little else for the remainder of the year. Many tree fruits fall into this category, for example. A big sign offering "Fresh Peaches," placed several yards down the road in each direction, would give drivers enough warning to slow down and stop.

For this direct, down-and-dirty approach, you can sell right off the tailgate of your pickup truck. Make certain, however, that you check local laws and regulations before you settle upon a location for your sales. Many jurisdictions require a permit for this type of selling. Even when no permit is needed, if you park on a public roadway, you can run afoul of all sorts of laws and ordinances, which might result in a costly ticket.

A better approach is to persuade a local business, such as a gas station or hardware store, to allow you to sell in their lot. I'd be leery of paying rent for such a privilege, as this will drastically reduce profits. Instead, point out to the owner or manager that your presence can increase his or her store traffic. Some vendors in my area simply choose a vacant lot, hoping the owner either won't mind the trespass, or is absent. In a busy retail zone, this may be the easiest way to find a spot. Provided, of course, that you meet permit requirements.

Set Up a Cart

A more sophisticated form of direct marketing may appeal to you, especially if you don't mind making a small, up-front investment. In many areas, you can become a street vendor by purchasing a permit from the local authorities and setting up a pushcart stand. From this venue, if you choose your street corner wisely, you could sell flowers, gourmet produce, cut and/or potted herbs, and/or seasonal decorative items with great success. Because of the investment, not to mention the time commitment, this approach makes little sense unless you are serious about earning a part-time income from your microfarm.

On-Site Selling

Farmers in rural areas have for years capitalized on the desire of folks to escape the city. Inviting customers to visit your home and purchase produce on the spot may be an option worth exploring, depending upon your circumstances.

First and foremost, you must live in an area zoned for this kind of activity. Many communities restrict such sales in residential areas. Some developments may prohibit home-based businesses through deed covenants. In these instances, you'd be wise not to break the rules.

If local regulations allow, however, you can often get full price for your products without having to truck them to the market by advertising for customers in the local paper and on bulletin boards. Make sure to clearly state hours of operation, or you'll have people showing up at the oddest times to buy veggies. Even with clearly stated hours, you may still get unexpected customers. Treat each as if they'd arrived during scheduled hours. Better to suffer a little inconvenience than to miss a sale. More importantly, if you accommodate such customers they may or may not praise you publicly, but if you turn someone away, they will complain to everyone they see about how rudely you treated them.

It would be foolish to invite the general public to visit without protecting yourself with liability insurance. A million dollars of liability protection would be the absolute minimum in these litigious times. Consult with an insurance professional, outlining your plans and the number of visitors you anticipate per month. Despite the drain on profits that an insurance premium represents, you cannot afford to "bet the farm" under any circumstances. When I formed my first corporation and opened a retail store, my lawyer told me I would be sued within the first five years, despite any precautions I might take. I scoffed at this privately until his prediction came true. Fortunately, I had followed his advice and purchased liability insurance. And we won the case.

Internet and Mail-Order Selling

Some farm products lend themselves to mail-order sales, and the Internet has revolutionized this market for the small operator. With minimal technical expertise, it is now possible to set up a web-based business, collect payments, and communicate with your clients, all for very little money. The trick, of course, is obtaining some visibility among the millions of other web pages out there.

The most obvious advantage of mail order is the ability to deal with customers on your schedule. Your Internet-based store is open 24-7. Even if you post a telephone number, you can always let the call go to voice mail, and most, if not all, of your correspondence will be via e-mail. Further, eliminating the need for customers to come to you automatically avoids one of the principle drawbacks to a home-based business in the suburbs, where the added traffic generated by a retail business is seldom welcome and frequently prohibited. The only traffic engendered by mail order is the UPS truck picking up your packages. UPS presumably visits your neighborhood anyway, and you can avoid even this bit of traffic by taking packages to the nearest drop-off point yourself.

Having operated two mail-order businesses in the days before the Internet, I can vouch for the huge benefits realized through not having to produce a paper catalog. While paper mail-order catalogs are hardly a thing of the past, you can promote conservation and save thousands of dollars by posting your catalog on the Internet instead. "The flower sells the plant" is an old saying in the nursery business. Thus, color photos are a must for a mail-order nursery, but digital technology has reduced the cost of producing and displaying them to the merest fraction of what it once was.

Mail-order selling places no limits on your potential market. There may be only one gardener in your home town willing to buy your specialty nursery stock, but you can reach thousands of like-minded people via a website.

Avoid Mail-Order Misfires

Admittedly, mail-order marketing has its drawbacks. There are extra expenses for packaging materials, and time is required to pack products so they won't suffer in transit. If you ship nursery stock, you must have a nursery license in your home state, or the recipient's state department of agriculture may not allow your shipment in. Some states, notably California and Hawaii, have especially stringent requirements in this regard, with the result that many mail-order houses will not ship to those states. Providing good customer service will demand some time, too. For example, dealing with the inevitable lost shipment can sometimes test your patience. You will also quickly discover that creating and maintaining a website requires a considerable commitment of time. You cannot just post a site and never change it again. Keeping your site's content and appearance fresh is essential to keep customers coming back.

Weigh these pros and cons carefully before you try mail order. Despite the drawbacks many growers have found it a profitable way to market specialty crops.

Community Supported Agriculture

Community Supported Agriculture (CSA) arrangements offer one of your best options for making money by growing vegetables. Customers typically pay an up-front fee in exchange for a weekly box of produce throughout the growing season. The advantage to the farmer is obvious: the customer base provides the capital you need for seeds and supplies. The consumer benefits by getting the freshest seasonal food without the hassle of going shopping. CSA arrangements have been around for years. This was one of the ways I sold veggies during the early 1990s. With more people becoming "locavores," the term coined to describe those who seek out local food, CSA programs are on the rise.

If your time is constrained for a lot of marketing chores, or you simply don't enjoy doing it, starting your own CSA service can turn your surplus vegetables into extra income with very little effort. Start by asking neighbors to become customers. Getting money up front for future product delivery is hard to beat, and knowing who your customers are simplifies planning your vegetable garden. Make sure to avoid the mistake of overselling your production capacity.

Who's There?

Most of the foregoing discussion has been concerned with identifying markets in the specific sense of outlets for the products of your suburban microfarm. Devoting some research time to locating these markets is essential to success, but you must also concern yourself with your customers and their needs and desires. *Who* is every bit as important as *where*. In order to bring your products to the attention of customers ready to buy them, you must know who your customers are.

For example, food ethnicity can be a big factor in landing sales. Many Asian cuisines call for specialty greens like tatsoi and mizuna. Latino cooks want fresh chilies. Income levels also correlate with food preferences. If you are charging premium prices, you are likely to sell more in an affluent neighborhood than in a less fortunate one. Decide to whom your products would most appeal and then apply common sense. Such considerations can be crucially important to the success of a microfarm, because the size of the operation demands the highest return possible on every square foot of growing space. Thus, you generally should strive to sell products that carry a high cost per unit—basil rather than parsley, for example. Further, you must generally sell at retail to obtain the best price. If you want to sell perennial cut flowers, for example, you could contact florists, caterers, and wedding planners, but these professionals will expect to pay the lower wholesale price. You can ask more money per stem at the farmers' market.

The ethnic, political, economic, and age composition of a community of people is known as the "demographics" of that community. You can use demographic information compiled for your community to target the most likely customers. Younger people, for example, may be more interested in organically grown food than their parents and grandparents. Wealthier customers are more likely to want "gourmet" items such as French beans and arugula, while blue-collar folks tend to gravitate toward potatoes and cabbage. This is not to imply that you should focus solely upon a one-market "segment," e.g., young people, white-collar workers, or whatever. Looking at the local demographics can give you basic insights into where your likely best customers can be found.

chapter three

Find the Ideal Product

Now that you have made your best guesses as to what the market wants, it's time to decide where to focus your efforts. Chances are you will develop your microfarm with multiple crops, integrating all your resources to achieve the annual sales goal you have established. To arrive at the proper product mix will be a task for each individual, but you can follow some basic guidelines.

Start with perennial plants that are already in place, such as a fruit tree or a border of cutting flowers. Estimate the annual income possible from the harvest of apples or spring bouquets. You probably have several such potential income sources. Arrive at estimates for each, and total up the amount of sales you think they will generate during the coming season. Subtracting the result from your goal leaves the amount you need to earn from sales of vegetables and/or annual flowers. We'll call those sales dollars "new sales."

Next, look at your sketches and figure out how many square feet you have available to produce more products. Dividing the annual goal for new sales by the area of this space gives you the productivity you need to reach your sales goal, in dollars per square foot. Armed with this number, you can proceed to create a crop plan.

Take a Long, Hard Look in the Mirror

Finding the right product mix for your microfarm means considering not merely what you can produce but, more importantly, what you can successfully sell. Selling vegetables, for example, can involve a lot of direct interaction with the purchaser. Customers at the farmers' market will want to know not only whether those unusual Asian greens are fresh but also to what culinary uses they might be best adapted. Prepare for this with a printed recipe or two.

Customers will engage you in discussions of your growing methods, offer their opinions about crop varieties, and almost always ask when to expect your first sweet corn or ripe peaches. If you find such extensive customer contact daunting, then perhaps you should focus more effort on selling nursery stock to a couple of local garden centers or find a few good chefs who will take most of your produce. You could also consider starting a CSA group.

Time constraints will play a crucial role in your decisions, too. If you already have a crowded schedule, you may not be able to spend time growing *and* marshaling a local sales effort. Or maybe your leisure time does not coincide with the optimum sales schedule; you have to work a regular job when the farmers' market is operating. In these situations selling via the Internet may make more sense, and you should choose a product that lends itself to this approach. You might, for example, develop an inventory of rare seeds or bulbs that are shipped during their winter dormancy rather than having to cope with perishable seasonal vegetables. The Internet has a highly developed community of avid gardeners, foodies, and herb enthusiasts. The possibilities for using these channels to test new ideas seem limitless. Internet sales also permit scaling your business to match your production capacity. When something is sold out, you can instantly remove it from your website, or perhaps invite customers to put themselves on a want list for next year's crop.

You must also ask yourself how far you want to go with your microfarm project. If adding value to a product is required to meet your sales goals, are you prepared to take that step? Say you realize that you can wring a higher dollar yield from an herb garden if you include packaged dried herbs in your offerings. Doing so, however, will require containers, labels, and a large dehydrator, plus the time to weigh and pack the finished product. Going the distance of actually creating a prepared food product, like pickles or jam, requires a commercial kitchen, health inspections, and product liability insurance. Is this *really* what you want to do? Do you have the capital for these endeavors? How long will it take to recoup that investment? You must answer these questions before you dig. You'd be wise to get assurances of the rest of the family's cooperation up front. You don't want to argue about who is going to help pick strawberries while the crop spoils in the patch. Would your annual trip to Mom's house in Florida coincide with the spring nursery sales season? Farming on any scale is to some extent a way of life, and starting a farm business will likely alter some of your accustomed patterns of family activity. Thinking about potential problems and conflicts now will save a lot of frustration later.

Examine your own likes and dislikes, the ways you prefer to spend your leisure time, and your enthusiasm for selling before settling on the direction your microfarm will take. For example, I prefer developing one-on-one relationships with a few carefully selected garden centers as an outlet for the rare plants I grow. The hurly-burly of retail sales at the farmers' market was more fun when I was younger and more inclined toward new adventures.

Good Neighbor Policies

Besides the needs of your family and your personal aspirations, consider also the people living around you. Keeping peace with the neighbors is an important aspect of suburban farming. The folks across the street might complain if yours is the only lawn replaced by a lettuce patch. One of the best ways to win a neighbor's approval is a gift of fresh vegetables. Leave a handwritten note in every bag of goodies inviting the recipient to visit you at the farmers' market, too.

Find the Best Product

Every possible product your microfarm might yield has its advantages and disadvantages. Thus, depending upon your particular situation, there are good and bad crop choices. To help sort them out, consider rating different possibilities according to these key criteria:

- **Productivity:** the amount of salable crop per square foot cultivated
- **Market value:** the price you can charge for a unit of crop
- **Estimated demand:** the volume of a crop you can reasonably expect to sell

- **Capital requirement:** the amount of money needed, for seed, fertilizer, and so forth, to bring in a crop
- **Personal zeal:** your familiarity with the cultivation of a crop, and the enthusiasm you bring to its production

The ideal crop is one that generates a lot of produce per square foot over the course of a season. It has a higher market value, and is in greater demand, than other possible crops that you can accommodate in the same space. Its capital requirement is an amount you can easily afford. The crop is one that you enjoy growing, and in which you can recognize and achieve top quality.

chapter four

What Do I Have? Evaluate Your Assets

Before you can decide how you can be successful with the microfarm concept, you need to evaluate what you have and figure out how you will employ it to the best advantage. Most people have tangible items, such as space, water, and equipment, as well as intangible assets, such as horticultural knowledge, an unusually favorable microclimate, or perhaps connections in the nursery business.

Tangible Assets

You can easily measure your tangible assets. Cash is the most basic tangible asset for all businesses. You are going to need a small amount of cash for start-up capital, mostly for things like fees, seeds, or advertising. We will cover these needs later. For now, let's consider what else you can bring to the table. The assets discussed in this chapter may not wind up on your balance sheet, but they are nevertheless of major importance to your success.

Space

Growing plants takes room. Do you have enough room to grow enough plants to make your efforts worthwhile? Further, how does your land lie? Is there sun or shade? Is it more or less level, or steeply inclined? Do existing barriers, such as an adjacent house, pose a problem? Can you gain more sun by pruning a large tree? The answers to these and many other similar questions will be site-specific and will to a considerable extent determine what you can grow for market.

Start with some stakes, a tape measure, and a sheet of graph paper, and lay out a rough scale drawing of your site. Use stakes to set benchmarks, then take a series of measurements from these points, recording the distances on the graph paper. A good place to begin is at a corner where your property adjoins your neighbor's. Work from that point around the circumference of your lot. As you go, indicate on your site plan large trees, outbuildings, your residence, and other significant features.

Next, study your drawing to identify areas that can be used for crop production. If you do a good job with the sketch, you can easily add up the number of square feet you have available to generate extra income. Let's say you have 2,000 square feet. Using a target of $10,000 in annual sales, it is apparent that each square foot must generate $5 annually. Knowing this limits your choices of possible crops to those that will deliver the necessary dollars in productivity.

Water

Agriculture requires water in copious quantities. Rain is the ideal primary water source, but it may not arrive in the appropriate amounts, or at the right times. Sooner or later, you will need to irrigate. Thus, you must consider not only the quantity but also the quality of available water.

If you happen to have a stream or lake adjacent, be sure to check with local authorities concerning withdrawal of irrigation water. Natural waters typically are subject to close government regulation, and you will probably need a permit. If you have a small pond, a cistern, or other means to capture and store rain water, this provides the perfect option for low-cost irrigation. For most suburban microfarmers, the municipal water supply will be the only option for irrigation.

Learn as much as you can from your monthly utility bill. How much does a gallon of water cost? How much do you pay for sewer service? The sewer charge can double your cost for a gallon of irrigation water, maybe increase it even more. However, some utilities provide ways around this, in the form of a "seasonal watering" credit, or "sewer charge rebate." The utility company may be willing to compare your winter water use with summer use, and to issue a credit for sewer charges on the difference. The justification is that water used for irrigation does not flow down the drain, so you are not using the sewer service to remove this water. My utility offers such a break but makes no effort to advertise it. To find a similar deal in your area, call the utility company.

Another option is to have a secondary meter installed. Such a meter provides a separate measure of the water used for irrigation. The utility company reads both meters, and subtracts the secondary meter reading from the sewer bill, so you pay only for the water. In some jurisdictions, it may be possible to install this meter yourself and enjoy a considerable savings over the fees (typically $500 to $1,000) charged by the utility company. In other jurisdictions, you have no DIY option. Regardless, you must calculate whether the investment is worth it. In my case, I found that only fourteen months would be required to cover the $625 cost of a secondary meter for a greenhouse.

Utilities measure water usage either in gallons, cubic feet, or hundred cubic feet. (One cubic foot of water equals 7.5 gallons.) The sewer charge is then based on water usage. Check with your supplier if you need help figuring out your bill.

How Much Water Do You Need?

Your water needs will vary depending upon the type of crop and method of cultivation. Vegetables growing in the open in raised beds will need irrigation only to supplement natural rainfall. Floral stock in a polyethylene greenhouse will have no other water source than the irrigation you provide. In the latter case, irrigation water can be more costly than the payments on the greenhouse. Estimate usage by calculating the irrigation needed to equal one inch of rainfall per week, a reasonable amount of water for most crop production.

Let's say you have 240 square feet of greenhouse bench space for growing fresh basil. One inch of rain over this space equals 20 cubic feet of water (240 divided by 12 inches per foot). That's 150 gallons per week, or 600 gallons per month. If the combined water and sewer charge is two cents per gallon (about what it costs in my town), you will pay $12 per month in utility charges to irrigate the basil crop.

Creating these estimates not only helps determine the profit potential of your microfarm but also provides the necessary data for deducting the utility charges from your farm income when tax time arrives.

Water quality may be an issue in the case of some crops. Orchids, carnivorous plants, and ferns, for example, are often fussy about the mineral content of their irrigation water. Because these are high-value crops, you may need to improve upon the existing water supply in order to produce them. A common water-quality issue is too much "hardness." This term refers to the quantity of dissolved mineral salts, particularly calcium and magnesium. Hard water can interfere with the adsorption of critical plant nutrients. A more mundane effect is the appearance of unsightly white or yellowish spots on plant leaves, telltale signs of hardness left behind when the water evaporates.

Reverse osmosis, a process whereby water is forced under pressure through a semipermeable plastic membrane, provides a practical way to purify irrigation water. For horticultural purposes, reverse osmosis is preferable to deionization, another common method, because the latter introduces sodium into the product water, replacing the hardness components. Plants generally abhor sodium. Reverse osmosis has its drawbacks, primarily the production of a considerable amount of waste water for each gallon of product.

If you need low-mineral water and reverse osmosis is not an attractive option, do what people have been doing for centuries: collect rainwater. You can buy plastic rain barrels at many garden centers or via mail order. Many are designed to attach easily to an existing downspout, with a bib near the bottom to connect a garden hose. Look for these additional features: a tight-fitting lid to prevent access by mosquitoes; a base that elevates the bottom of the barrel a bit, allowing it to be drained completely; built-in fittings that permit more than one barrel to be connected in series. You can sometimes obtain plastic barrels free or inexpensively and convert them to rain storage. If you recycle a used barrel, make sure the original contents consisted of something completely harmless.

Time

That "time is money" is a cliché. The profit you realize at the end of each season is the only monetary compensation you can expect for your time spent weeding, watering, and digging. Accordingly, having enough time to spare for these chores is an essential asset. A micro-farm will lengthen your to-do list, to be sure. If you must spend less time at other pursuits in order to tend the farm, watching less TV or playing fewer video games might be a reasonable way to free up some time. Refusing to work overtime at your regular job might be unwise. Besides meeting our commitments, we all need time to spend with family and friends, to toss sticks for the dog, or to read a book. It would be a mistake to forgo any of these activities merely to earn a little extra money.

If you don't have a lot of spare time for gardening, some of the most efficient crops are field-grown nursery stock, small fruits, and herbs. They may be seasonally demanding, but seldom do these crops require daily care. At the other end of the spectrum lie gourmet vegetables, orchids, and cut flowers. These crops may command your attention more than once per day. The trade-off in these cases is the return on investment. The most time-consuming crops also carry the highest value. Thus, a realistic and careful assessment of the time you have available must be part of the plan for your microfarm. One of the greatest benefits of creating a microfarm is that you can design it around most constraints. There is no set path to success. With a little planning, you can earn money doing something you enjoy with whatever leisure time you have available.

Stock Plants

If you are already an avid gardener, chances are you have many plants that can provide a crop. I use a simple database program to keep track of the various plant varieties in my garden, together with as much additional information as I decide is pertinent to crop production. You may want to begin your microfarm project by assembling a stock plant inventory.

If you plan to sell cut flowers or nursery stock, take pictures of your stock plants in bloom. Images, you will discover, are essential to most of the various forms of marketing you may undertake as a suburban farmer. Nurs-

PHOTO BY JOHN TULLOCK

Shoot images that will help sell your products

ery stock is a tough sale when it's not in bloom, but a sign with a color photo of the plant in flower can turn that situation around. You do not need professional quality images for signage or posting online. If you do not already own a digital camera, I suggest you purchase one and start recording the bounty of your microfarm as soon as possible.

Intangible Assets

Assets that are difficult to measure and quantify are "intangible." People instinctively notice, and are drawn to, freshness, attractiveness, vigor, and all the other signs of good health in plants, produce, and flowers. Your ability to achieve these qualities in the crops you produce is your most important intangible asset.

Favorable Microclimate

You can remedy almost any shortcoming of your property, in terms of agricultural production, with the sole exception of sun exposure. If you haven't enough sun, some plants simply won't grow, and a great many will perform poorly. That said, numerous profitable nursery crops can be produced in the shade. Thus, you should consider carefully the sun exposure in the areas you propose to use for production. Besides the number of hours of sun a location receives per day during the growing season, exposure will affect how quickly or slowly the site's temperature changes with the changing seasons, its relationship to prevailing winds, and consequently its susceptibility to unseasonal weather.

It is common knowledge that an east-facing slope will warm up earlier in the spring than a west-facing one. Therefore, plants that are subject to damage from late spring frosts may benefit from later emergence when planted on the west side of a house. When planted on the east side, the same species may break dormancy too early and be damaged by a cold snap. Such differences in microclimate can determine whether your produce is ready earlier or later than normal for your area. Given that prices are often higher at the extremes of the season, desirable exposure can be highly valuable.

As you create your site drawing, locate north using a compass or GPS device and note the exposure of each of your proposed growing areas. If you have seasonal shade from a large deciduous tree, indicate the shade line on your drawing. Think about how to exploit conditions in each of these areas to achieve your production goals.

Knowledge

I doubt you'd be reading this book in the first place if you were not already a gardener.

- Have you developed a special talent for getting orchids to bloom?
- Do you grow the biggest, juiciest tomatoes on the block?
- Which of the varieties you currently grow perform best and most reliably?

A friend of mine dotes on hybrid tea roses, ignoring the old-fashioned climbing varieties on his alley fence. Yet blooms of the latter would sell, too, if only he'd cut them. The last thing you want, of course, is to base your plans on a variety that presents special challenges in your region of the country. Count your special knowledge of the plant kingdom as an asset, but do not focus solely on plants that interest you.

Do not despair if you lack gardening expertise. It does not require much effort to learn, and I will try to provide a basic education in the pages that follow. The key is to be open to a certain way of looking at the world. In my experience, the most capable gardeners all seem to share only one trait: extraordinary powers of observation. They are in touch with their gardens on all sensory channels. The smell of the warming earth, the trill of a woodpecker, the elegant symmetry of a dicentra blossom, the wriggling of an earthworm scooped up in a handful of soil—from each of these the exceptional gardener takes a lesson, weaving every observation into a rich fabric of understanding of intertwined relationships. If all you see in a patch of lettuce is dollar bills, you overlook the essentials of the movement you are striving to become a part of. If you can be the kind of farmer who senses that the work evokes something more important than merely selling food, you are on the proper track.

chapter five

Get Ready to Dig
Pay Dirt

If you have followed my suggestions thus far, you know what you can grow and where you can sell it. Now you need a business plan to keep you on track—yes, even for a business as small as your backyard. The surest way to reach your sales goal is to *plan* for success. Making a business plan need not be daunting.

Five basic elements make up a business plan. They are:

- A **mission statement** that explains the objectives of the proposed business in one sentence, or at most a short paragraph
- A **statement of goals** that names specific, usually financial- or sales-based targets and sets a definite time period to reach those targets
- A **financial plan** that incorporates the basic financial documents used by all businesses
- A **market analysis,** listing the markets you have identified for the products you plan to sell and the percentage of your total sales you expect each market to provide
- A **competition analysis** that identifies as many of your competitors as possible, together with what you perceive to be their strengths and weaknesses

On a Mission, with Goals

While each of these elements is important, the mission and goals statements should receive your attention first, as they will empower you to execute your plan. The mission statement presents the big picture, while the statement of goals tells you how to get there. A mission statement might read "We will earn $10,000 in additional annual income by growing tropical orchids in a small greenhouse." An example of a goal might be "We will sell 200 budded *Phalaenopsis* at $10 each to local garden centers between January 1 and June 1." Several such goals will likely be required to encompass your business objectives, because you will probably have to diversify to succeed. Whatever your particular situation might be, it is difficult to overestimate the value of having precisely articulated goals. If, instead of designating a clearly defined objective, I merely said, "We are going to sell perennials next year," I would leave a lot of questions unanswered. How many pots and how much soil mix will I need? Do I have enough stock plants to divide or will I have to buy starts of some varieties? When should the plants be developing flower buds? I can't answer any of these by referring to the vaguely worded statement. But the more specific statement of a goal provides the answers to all.

Distillation of all the information about your business into a list of briefly stated goals helps keep you anchored in reality. In my experience, it is all too easy to get distracted while trying to keep all the balls in the air. You may already have a job, family obligations, and a dozen other things vying for your time. If you are going to embark upon a small business venture with any hope of financial reward, you need to stay focused. For me, the best way to cope is to break the big task of "running the business" into a group of smaller tasks, such as "sell 500 one-gallon perennials."

Analyzing the Market and Your Competitors

You will need to do some research to analyze the available markets and the nature of the competition in your area. For starters, decide what "your area" means. Ask questions like:

- Are you willing to drive twenty miles to a farmers' market?
- How about 100 miles?
- How many garden centers does your county support?
- What kind of attendance should you expect at a particular market on Saturdays?
- Who supplies the florist in your neighborhood with sunflowers?

You can obtain such information in many ways.

"Click, call, or go," summarizes my approach to research. Look on the Internet, check the Yellow Pages, or just keep your eyes open along your daily commute route. (Pay attention to your driving, though!) An excursion to your nearest farmers' market should provide ideas, contacts, and an assessment of the customer base. Visit every garden center in the area to find potential customers for your plants.

Take three basic steps:

- Define the geographic location and size of your market area.
- Bring together the available data on all the possible outlets for your products.
- Form a good idea of the nature of your competition.

Now study this information and come up with three lists. The first will provide answers to the question "Who will buy my product?" The second list will answer "What venues exist to reach those customers?" The third list will state the competition's most obvious weaknesses. It will identify the "holes" in the current market that you think you can fill. For example, "None of the other vendors at my nearest farmers' market is selling arugula." Cite evidence from your research to support your contentions in the market and competition analysis sections of your business plan.

Money's the Main Object

The financial plan constitutes the heart of your business plan, because the overall objective is, of course, to turn a profit. The financial plan will answer the following basic questions:

- Can I make a profit on this venture?
- How much money will I need to invest?
- How long will it take to recover that investment?
- How much net income will this venture generate per year?

The financial plan consists of four documents: the **balance sheet**, the **profit and loss statement**, the **budget**, and the **cash flow analysis**. Each can be set up in a simple spreadsheet program, or you can purchase software with these documents already set up. As long as the financial data you include are accurate (or consist of your best estimates where accuracy is not possible) it makes no difference by what method you keep track of your assets, liabilities, expenses, and income. But you will need records, and it is worthwhile to follow long-established customs when opening a set of books. Furthermore, a well-kept set of business records can be mined for all sorts of valuable data. An examination of the function of each document in detail shows how useful they are, even for a microfarm business.

The Balance Sheet

A balance sheet is a "snapshot" of the value of a business at a specific point in time. Comparing two balance sheets prepared at different times allows you to determine if the business's value, or "net worth," is increasing or decreasing. Despite the small size of a backyard venture, you should prepare a balance sheet at least once a year. Otherwise, you won't know if the time spent on your business is being rewarded. Prepare your balance sheet by first listing all the business assets in a single column. Assets are things of value that the business will use in its quest for profits, including cash, money the business is owed, equipment, buildings, and inventory. You might, for example, open a business checking account with an initial deposit of $100. This amount goes in the asset column of the balance sheet.

A backyard business may involve few assets other than cash, especially at the outset. At the beginning, you will have made no sales and thus no money will be owed from customers.

SAMPLE BALANCE SHEET			
Assets:		Liabilities:	
Cash	$1,044.23	Accounts Payable	
Accounts Receivable		Notes Payable	$1,000
Inventory	$599.50	Total Liabilities	$1,000
Equipment, Used	$1,000.00	Net Worth	$1,643.73
Less Accumulated Depreciation	$ —	Total Liabilities and Net Worth	$2,643.73
Total Assets	$2,643.73		

As for equipment, you probably already own most of what you need. Keeping track of small items may not be worth the trouble, but if you want to include used hand tools, garden hoses, sprayers, and such, I suggest you lump all of these under a single asset account named "Small Equipment." Estimate the value of each item at the time you place it in service for your business. A good rule of thumb here is to set the value at whatever price you would ask for the item if you were selling it in a yard sale.

Larger items of equipment should be listed as assets, especially if they are new, or relatively so, because you get a tax deduction for the decrease in their value with use. This decrease is known as "depreciation," and it, too, appears on the balance sheet. Do you have a small lawn tractor and accessories? How about a vehicle for making deliveries? Do you plan to build a small greenhouse for business use? How about purchasing a portable building for storage or to use as a potting shed? For any of these items you should keep a record of the following information:

- Name of the item
- Date of purchase
- Purchase price
- Date placed in service for the business
- The item's fair market value on that date
- Extent of business use

I find it convenient to create a spreadsheet with this information for each item purchased for the business or placed into business service. The "extent of business use" entry above refers to things that have both business and personal use, such as a vehicle. Having this information for each piece of equipment will allow you to calculate the annual depreciation for that item when you prepare your tax returns. The IRS provides depreciation tables in the instructions for Form 4562, which is used to report depreciation on your tax return. You can estimate depreciation costs without reference to the tables. All of the equipment you will use in your backyard farm is considered to have a life span for depreciation purposes of five years. Dividing the purchase price (for a new item) or fair market value (for used items) by five gives the annual depreciation. If a piece of equipment is placed in service later in the year than January, the depreciation for the first year is reduced proportionately. For example, for an item placed in service on July 1, the depreciation would be reduced by half for that year, because it was not used for business purposes for the first half of the year.

Similarly, if you have equipment used for both business and nonbusiness purposes, such as a computer used partly for managing your business website and partly for personal e-mail, you may deduct only the portion of the depreciation corresponding to the percent of business use.

A car or truck provides a special case. For a microfarm operation, you likely will use your personal car for making deliveries to customers, rather than having a vehicle dedicated solely to business use. In this situation, most people will find it more advantageous to deduct business mileage rather than compute depreciation. The IRS sets an allowable per-mile deduction that takes into account depreciation, maintenance, and fuel costs, everything except parking fees and tolls. To take advantage of this deduction, keep a mileage log in the vehicle and record the beginning and ending odometer reading each time you take a business-related trip. You will be surprised at the end of the year how those weekly trips to the farmers' market can add up.

Consider with care the total amount of noncash assets you assign to your business. In some jurisdictions, you may be assessed a tax on the value of property held for business use. Sometimes the tax authority will grant an exemption for small, home-based operations. This is the case where I live. Business assets totaling under $1,000 in value are taxed at a nominal rate, and the business is exempt from filing detailed reports. Therefore, claiming new vehicle as a business asset, for example, could add to your tax burden. Not listing your car as a business asset normally would not prevent you from taking the mileage deduction for business use of a personal vehicle.

The tax structure where you live is likely to be different from mine. Check with a professional familiar with your local tax laws before you decide how to handle such assets.

After listing all your assets, create a second list of liabilities. Liabilities are amounts of money owed or committed for a specific business purpose. The simplest kind of liability involves purchases on credit. For example, using a credit card to buy potting mix for your nursery plants creates a liability. You will be paying off the credit card with the proceeds of the sale of the plants, hopefully. Until that time, you carry the amount as a liability on your balance sheet.

Totaling up the amounts in the assets and liabilities columns and finding the difference determines your business's "net worth." If the total value of your business assets exceeds the total of your liabilities, the net worth is a positive number. As your business grows, you want to see that net worth increase over time. Changes in net worth occur because of changes in the money inflows to, and outflows from, the business. These money flows are called, respectively, "income" and "expenses." Keeping track of them is essential. For that, we need another financial document, the profit and loss statement.

The Profit and Loss Statement

The profit and loss statement is a summary of the business's income and expenses for a specific period of time. Businesses typically prepare this statement on a monthly, quarterly, and annual basis. To prepare the statement you add up your income, subtract your expenses, and the difference is your profit for the time period under consideration. If you sell 500 one-gallon perennials for a total income of $2,500 and your cost for plants, pots, fertilizer, and potting media was $500, your gross profit on this sale is $2,000. A profit and loss statement summarizes all such income and costs for the business operation. Costs of production, such as the pots, are known as "direct" costs.

Besides pots and potting mix, you may have had expenses for gas to heat your greenhouse, in order to produce the 500 perennials.

Chances are, the greenhouse was used for other plants besides the perennials. Costs such as these, spread over the entire operation of the business and not attributable to any one product, are known as "indirect" costs. Other common indirect costs are advertising, utilities, and office expenses such as postage, paper products, and printer cartridges.

PROFIT AND LOSS STATEMENT	
January 1 to December 31	
INCOME:	
Sales—Nursery Stock	$10,465.00
Sales—Produce	$526.00
Sales—Cut Flowers	$380.00
Less Refunds Given	($25.00)
TOTAL SALES	$11,346.00

EXPENSES:	
Vehicle Mileage @ $0.45/mile	$216.00
Chemicals	$ —
Depreciation	$ —
Fertilizer	$35.00
Fuel for Garden Tractor	$62.00
Insurance	$ —
Interest	$ —
Labor	$ —
Repairs	$ —
Seeds and Plants Purchased	$88.00
Supplies	$ —
Taxes and Fees	$128.00
Utilities	$332.00
Other Expenses	$ —
TOTAL EXPENSES	$861.00
Net Profit	$10,485.00

Every business owner should keep careful records for the profit and loss statement. Not only will crunching the numbers each month tell you whether or not the business is making money, but every expense is also a potential tax deduction.

I find it helpful to arrange my profit and loss statement to correspond with the categories on Schedule F of IRS Form 1040. You must file Schedule F to report farm income. For example, on Schedule F you separately report sales of items you bought for resale and items you sold that you also grew. You should, therefore, keep a separate tally of both classes of products. (The form lists some other income categories, but these are not likely to apply to a backyard farm operation.)

I prefer to know the amount of income generated by each species and cultivar in my inventory, and so I keep a separate accounting of sales by species. This practice consumes more time than merely lumping all your sales together, but I learned quickly that some species are "bread and butter" while others are plain "losers." Because the resources of a backyard business are necessarily limited, you cannot afford to waste them on the losers, and it therefore behooves you to compile the data.

Schedule F categorizes farm expenses as follows:

- Car and truck
- Chemicals
- Custom hire
- Depreciation
- Employee benefits
- Feed
- Fertilizers
- Gasoline
- Insurance
- Interest
- Labor
- Pension plans
- Rent
- Repairs
- Seeds and plants
- Storage
- Supplies
- Taxes
- Utilities
- Veterinary
- Other

As with all things tax-related, exceptions and rules apply to these categories. Some of the categories simply won't apply to your operation. If you have no employees other than yourself, you can obviously dispense with categories for employee benefits, labor costs, and pension plans.

Tax Considerations

The mere fact of owning a home-based business may confer tax advantages. Items not formerly deductible become so when they can be shown to have a business purpose. Thus, the interest on financing a hobby greenhouse, together with the cost of water and other utilities to operate it, plus its depreciation, may become at least partially deductible if you sell plants grown in that greenhouse.

I am neither an accountant nor a tax expert, and am speaking only from my personal experience, not offering legal or tax advice. Because each situation is unique, make certain to consult a professional before making decisions that might affect your taxes.

Note that losses sustained from a farming operation can in some instances be deducted from your other income. For example, suppose you note that nursery stock is selling well at your farmers' market. During the summer you decide that next season you will sell some day lily plants in addition to vegetables. You purchase some potting supplies, and by fall you have 1,000 pots of day lilies, divisions from the most prized varieties in your extensive collection. Although these plants are likely to sell like hotcakes next June when they bloom, you won't earn a dime on them by the end of December. In fact, you'll have to keep them watered during an unusually dry winter season. Nevertheless, all the expenses related to these plants can be deducted on your Schedule F, to reduce your other income from vegetable sales. If the overall operation has a loss, despite the vegetable sales, you can deduct this loss from your total taxable income.

For more information regarding the tax implications of your microfarm business, go to *www.irs.gov* and download IRS Publication 225, Farmer's Tax Guide.

Labor Costs

Even though a microfarm is unlikely to require full-time employees, you might occasionally need to hire someone to help with the chores. Unless you need a lot of help, don't fret that having a part-time employee may result in payroll taxes and tons of paperwork. According to the IRS, you can pay a casual worker or workers up to $600 per year without documentation. That includes your college-age son, or the kid down the street. However, once your expenses for this kind of labor exceed $600, you are required to file more forms.

Having actual employees on a regular basis will require you not only to withhold and deposit income and social security tax payments for each person but also to match their contributions to social security and Medicare. In order to justify not only the costs in payroll taxes but also the time spent keeping records and filing with the government, your business must enjoy significant sales. If you anticipate needing a labor force, therefore, you'd better make sure family members are willing to pitch in before you plant the first seed.

The Budget

A budget is nothing more than a hypothetical profit and loss statement. Prior to your first year of operation, for example, you will be mostly guessing when you try to assign numbers to the expense and income categories set up for your record keeping. In doing so, you will create a budget. Use it, together with the records you amass as your operation proceeds, as a yardstick against which to measure the accuracy of your predictions, with the goal of producing a more refined budget for next year.

A good budget document should set limits on where you will take your business for a specified period into the future. This may at first sound as though you are holding back or passing up opportunities. On the contrary, it is more likely that your business will suffer more from *unplanned* growth than from a plan that is too conservative. Look at it this way: It might be nice to know that you could sell forty crates of tomatoes a week to your local gourmet specialty market, but you will have to hire help to produce and deliver those tomatoes. You will need to buy 400 empty crates over a ten-week period. By the time you consider all the costs, the deal may turn out to be a loser. You can discover this only by preparing a budget for increasing tomato production.

A budget not only helps you forecast the implications of a business move, it also keeps a lid on spending. In my nursery business, it would be easy to overspend on stock plants, for example. Thus, I have a budget amount set aside for stock plants, and I spend no more than that each year.

One of the best ways to generate a budget when you don't have a previous year's data to go on is to start with your sales goal and work backward. For example, throughout this book our basic sales goal is $10,000 for the selling season. If I am selling perennials for which I can expect to receive an average price of $5 per plant, then I will need to sell 2,000 plants to achieve my goal. Allowing for a 10 percent loss rate means I will need 2,222 plants in all. (I plan to sell 90 percent of the plants I start out with, and I need to sell 2,000 plants. Therefore, I need to grow 2,000/0.9, or 2,222 plants.) Let's round it up and call it 2,225 plants. If they are to be in "trade gallon" containers, the usual way perennials are sold, I need 2,225 containers, and about twenty-two bales of my preferred brand of potting mix. Along with this, I will need thirty-five pounds of timed-release fertilizer, assuming I add one-quarter ounce to each pot. Anything else? Oh, yes, the plants themselves, about half of which I will start from seed. The remainder I will purchase from a supplier in Texas. If I buy 1,000 small plants for 65 cents apiece, the cost will be $650 plus shipping, and seeds for the remainder will be about $25.

And so forth.

In this manner, you can create a budget that will account for the expenses associated with producing the plants and getting them to market.

The Cash Flow Analysis

Cash flow analysis takes the budgeting process to the next level by imposing upon it the dimension of time. For example, the first year of a nursery business selling perennial plants may be mostly expense and little income. Nevertheless, the suppliers of pots, media, and plants will expect to be paid. This means you will be laying out cash for these items early in the life of the crop, and only when it is sold will you replace that cash with the proceeds of those sales. To make matters worse, if you are selling wholesale to the local garden center, the customer may expect you to extend credit, at least for thirty days. Retail businesses like to pay all their bills at the end of the month, when the coffers, presumably, are bulging from the preceding days of brisk sales. (They might also do this because the bookkeeper only looks at the bills once a month!) This means you may be potting up plants in August that will not provide you with any revenue until next July. *Voilà*! You have a cash flow problem. Anticipating such situations is the purpose of a cash flow analysis.

I suggest you develop a cash flow analysis for at least twelve months of operation. Using a spreadsheet, assign a column to each of the next twelve months. On the first row for a month, enter the amount of cash on hand in the checking account. The subsequent rows will correspond to individual income or expense items, such as "Sales, Ferns" or "Potting Mix" for each month. Try to anticipate all such items you may encounter during the forthcoming year. Estimate amounts as accurately as possible. With spreadsheet software, of course, you can always make changes where necessary.

When filling in the data for expenses, enter the amount as a negative number. Done this way, each column can be summed to find the cash balance at the end of the month. That number becomes the beginning balance for the first of the following month. A typical cash flow analysis spreadsheet for four months might look like the spreadsheet on the next page.

As you complete the spreadsheet for a full year of operations, you will note that the "Net Cash" balance fluctuates. It may even dip into negative territory now and then. Estimating your cash flow shows you when those low and high points can be expected. This gives you a chance to figure out how to deal with those nasty negative numbers before the fact. (Hint: You will have to pump more money in at those times.) It should be obvious that a clear understanding of the effect of cash flow can make or break your microfarm business. If you run out of money for fertilizer before the crop is ready, for example, you are, to use the technical term, "toast."

CASH FLOW ANALYSIS				
March Through June				
ITEM	MARCH	APRIL	MAY	JUNE
BEGINNING BALANCE	$1,250.00	$73.75	$2,189.75	$8,471.75
Sales—Nursery Stock	$375.00	$4,528.00	$5,782.00	$743.00
Sales—Produce	$75.00	$650.00	$850.00	$787.00
Sales—Cut Flowers	$0.00	$100.00	$250.00	$312.00
Refunds	$0.00	($75.00)	$0.00	$0.00
Pots and Potting Mix	($1,455.25)	($2,622.00)	$0.00	$0.00
Seeds and Plants	($36.00)	($250.00)	($325.00)	$0.00
Fuel For Garden Tractor	($10.00)	$0.00	($10.00)	($14.00)
Taxes and Fees	($20.00)	$0.00	$0.00	($100.00)
Water Bill	($105.00)	($215.00)	($265.00)	($385.00)
NET CASH	$73.75	$2,189.75	$8,471.75	$9,819.75

What's Your Return on Investment?

Your return at the end of the year should be greater than it would have been had you invested your capital in something else. Let's say you want to start your business with $1,000 your brother gave you for your birthday. You could have put the money in a savings account instead of buying nursery supplies. That might earn you 3 percent, or $30. Maybe you could earn 7 percent, or $70, by investing in the stock market. If at the end of the year you have $1,100 left over in the garden business checking account, you have earned

$100, or 10 percent, and the microfarm has turned out to be a better investment than either of the other options. This simplistic example does not take into account your labor, but it illustrates the point.

If you borrow money for the business, you must deduct the interest paid from the profits before determining the rate of return. This effectively raises the return on investment threshold by the interest rate percentage. For example, instead of using a birthday gift, suppose you take a cash advance on your Visa card. If the card's annual percentage rate is 9 percent, and you could have made 3 percent by putting the money in a savings account, the business must return more than 12 percent on this money in order to be considered a good investment.

Put It All Together

Creating a business plan for your new microfarm need not be a daunting task. Here are the three basic things you need to do:

- Create a mission statement, statement of goals, market analysis, competition analysis, and financial plan.
- Develop a balance sheet, profit and loss statement, and budget and cash flow analysis, covering a period of at least one year.
- Create and follow a business plan to help keep you on track when multiple obligations place demands on your time.

Keep this important point in mind: The effort to create a plan is wasted if you leave it on your hard drive and don't look at it again. A good business plan should be subject to constant revision. Review it monthly, determine if you are meeting your goals, and make any necessary adjustments. By modifying your business plan as circumstances require, you can steer your backyard farm toward its maximum profitability.

chapter six

Now, Make It Happen!

Launching a microfarm puts you in the plant business. Like other living things, plants have more or less inflexible requirements that must be respected if you expect to get results. Furthermore, the market restricts what sells and when. Poinsettias sell at Christmas. Pumpkins interest no one after autumn has come and gone. Timing is everything in the plant business. That is why the emphasis thus far has been on careful planning and research.

In the chapters that follow, I will summarize the essential information needed by every would-be suburban farmer, organized according to the type of crop. My aim is to help even those with no basic knowledge of gardening. As noted already, your microfarm will most likely not subsist upon a single crop but will depend upon a succession of crops throughout the season. However, horticultural information applies to all types of crops. Because the essence of the new urban farm movement is not only to produce food locally but also to do so with the least possible impact on the environment, it is essential for you to comprehend natural farming methods, and the many reasons why they are good for the planet.

Farming Nature's Way

On our small family farm, my grandfather practiced many of today's organic techniques, such as composting and cover-cropping. Granddad did not consider himself an organic farmer, though. Pesticides and chemical fertilizers were to him merely expensive luxuries, not threats to the environment. Indeed, the most "modern" organic methods are as old as agriculture itself. Organic fertilizers have been used for centuries. Native Americans advised the early colonists to bury a fish in each hill of corn seeds, for example.

Organic: Out of the Closet

In the 1960s, interest in organic growing methods became linked to vegetarianism, environmentalism, and the back-to-nature movement. Practices such as composting, recycling, and natural pest control unfortunately languished on the fringes of agriculture, while factory farms flourished with the help of millions of tons of chemicals. Today, however, natural farming methods are mainstream.

Even convenience stores stock a few organic products. At upscale markets like Earth Fare and Whole Foods, the coffee and vanilla are not only organic, they are also labeled "fair trade." Many Americans have come to view agriculture in the larger context of a sociopolitical movement that seeks to improve the human condition, while preserving the Earth's irreplaceable ecosystems that sustain all life. Some farmers refer to this view of agriculture as "beyond organic."

The Silent Springboard to a Better Way

Rachel Carson, with her landmark 1962 book, *Silent Spring*, awakened the consciousness of a generation to the dangers of chemical pesticide use in agriculture. Carson was a talented marine biologist, but it was her gifts as an author that led to her involvement with pesticide controversies. She wrote a marvelously lyrical trilogy about the oceans and the life within them, *The Sea Around Us*, *The Edge of the Sea*, and *Under the Sea Wind*. She might have gone on to write more nature books, but events intervened that changed the direction of her writing.

In 1957, the USDA began a fire ant eradication program. It involved the aerial spraying of both public and private property with DDT and other toxic chemicals. Opposition to the program was intense in some affected communities, and a lawsuit seeking to halt the spraying program made it all the way to the U.S. Supreme Court. The court ruled in favor of the USDA, but opponents continued to fight. Carson was recruited by the Audubon Society to write about the dangers to human health and the environment from the wanton application of chemical pesticides. The result, published in 1962 as *Silent Spring*, provided a founding manifesto for the modern environmental movement. DDT was soon banned, and Congress eventually created the Environmental Protection Agency. Carson assembled a persuasive case for the damage wrought. She argued not for a wholesale ban on pesticide use, as is often claimed, but for a more reasoned, targeted approach to dealing with pests, including the deployment of biological controls and the limited application of chemicals when no other course of action would achieve the necessary results.

Just Say "No" to Chemical Pesticides

Few human activities hold the potential for environmental damage like that of the wholesale application of chemical poisons to millions of acres of farmland. *Silent Spring* reported devastating effects on birds and other wildlife and raised the specter of human cancers induced by food-borne chemical contaminants. Since the 1960s, many American farmers have confronted the danger and substantially reduced pesticide use. Some may have been motivated by ecological concerns, while others may simply have sought less-costly methods of protecting their crops. Nevertheless, many crops are still produced under a haze of chemical sprays. Among the more heavily affected vegetable crops are celery, lettuce, peppers, potatoes, and spinach. Among the least affected are asparagus, broccoli, cabbage, corn, onions, and peas. Consumers have demonstrated that they are willing to pay more for pesticide-free produce, sometimes as much as 100 percent more.

Rule Number One for the backyard farmer, therefore, is "No chemical pesticides." This does not mean you lack an arsenal of methodologies for protecting your crops—quite the contrary. It does mean you are protecting yourself, your customers, and your local ecosystems from harmful chemical contamination. You will be helping to conserve precious oil reserves. And you will decrease your cost of production, thus increasing profits.

You Have Alternatives

Both productivity and appearance are impaired when vegetable crops are attacked by pests. Your best insurance against pest damage is proper cultural techniques. Crops that are starved for any of the essentials (light, water, fertilizer, and air) become significantly more susceptible to insects and diseases. Therefore, your first line of defense must be working knowledge of plants and their needs. Other elements of natural farming, which we will discuss later in this chapter, include increasing soil fertility through wise crop plans and the use of compost. When pests show up despite proper culture, the natural farmer can turn to a suite of techniques collectively known as "integrated pest management," also discussed below.

Earth, Water, Air, Fire

Long before modern chemistry and physics were developed, humans recognized four basic elements: earth, water, air, and fire. And as ancient farmers must have done, modern natural farmers seek to achieve the proper combination of these four "elements" (with the sun's energy taking the place of fire) to bring a crop to fruition with the least trouble and expense. Understanding the role of the four elements in agriculture first requires a little knowledge of how plants work.

Photosynthesis is the process by which green plants take carbon dioxide from the *air* and combine it with *water* to create sugar. The energy for this process comes from *sunlight*. To build their cellular structures and carry out the biochemical "magic" of photosynthesis, plants require *earth*, or more specifically minerals derived from the Earth's rocks. If the farmer supplies all these elements consistent with the plant's needs, the plant can complete its life cycle and yield a crop. Imbalances among the four elements, or a shortage of any one of them, will inevitably lead at best to a reduction in productivity, and at worst, to crop failure.

Sunlight, since it provides all the energy for the farm's productivity, is the most important factor. Only a few vegetables can be grown at all with less than six hours daily of full sun exposure. In my experience, at least eight hours of sun are required for decent production levels, and even more is better. Since you can provide no economical substitute for sunlight, its availability should be your first consideration in locating your vegetable patch. Even a gravel parking area in full sun offers more potential for vegetable production than good soil in the shade. You can import soil, water, and nutrients, but you cannot truck in the sun.

Next to sunlight, the availability of water is of crucial importance. Vegetable production requires prodigious quantities of water, approximately one inch per week of precipitation or the equivalent irrigation. One inch of rain over 1,200 square feet of growing area equals 100 cubic feet of water. One hundred cubic feet is equal to

750 gallons. Depending upon the rainfall and the cost of water in your area, irrigation can be a significant farm expense. In some regions, it is the major cost.

At least the air is free. Your vegetable plants will be able to get all the carbon dioxide they need without much in the way of your assistance. However, your efforts at keeping plants pest free without pesticides will be much easier if you allow plenty of space between plantings for air circulation. Too much crowding encourages pests such as fungi to gain a foothold. Since the goal of your farming operation is marketable produce, you will need to allow enough space for each crop. The less damage your produce receives from pests, the better it will sell, and simply giving your crops some elbow room will help in this regard. Don't assume that you can increase productivity by closer spacing. Crowding plants is more likely to have the opposite effect.

Much ado is often made about the plant's relationship to the fourth basic element, earth (minerals). Discussions of micronutrients and trace elements, daunting to the chemistry challenged, often leave gardeners confused. Here's the skinny on the subject.

Elementary, My Dear Nitrogen

Plants require three major elements: nitrogen, phosphorus, and potassium, usually abbreviated "NPK." (The "K" is the chemical symbol for potassium, derived from the Latin word, *kalium*, which for obscure reasons has been retained by chemists for hundreds of years.) Of these, the one in shortest supply is nitrogen. Although it makes up about 80 percent of the atmosphere, nitrogen gas cannot be used by plants. It must be "fixed," that is, converted into a chemical form that plants can absorb, before it is usable. The natural forces that produce fixed nitrogen are lightning, volcanic eruptions, and especially the metabolic activities of certain types of bacteria. Without the latter, agriculture as we know it would not exist. Indeed, terrestrial plants would be far less widespread on the planet, and herbivores, perhaps, would never have evolved. That's how important fixed nitrogen is.

Today, much of the fixed nitrogen used in agriculture is produced by chemical processes and incorporated into the familiar fertilizer formulations you see lining the shelves of garden centers. Chemical fertilizer was invented by the German chemist Justus von Liebig (1803–1873). Liebig's discoveries in the area of plant metabolism led him to downplay the importance of other soil components, such as humus. Liebig maintained that plants need *only* N, P, and K, and his ideas fostered the chemical-based agriculture that continues to dominate the world's food producing activities.

At least initially, before your soil has developed fertility through repeated additions of compost and other organic fertilizers, it may prove difficult to provide enough nitrogen without resorting to the use of chemicals. In my view, which is shared by many, the judicious use of chemical fertilizer *in concert with other organic gardening techniques*, represents a reasonable compromise between practicality and sustainability. Your long-term goal, however, should be the eventual elimination of all chemicals by building up the soil using natural methods.

Compost Rules!

To the plant, it makes no difference whether its fixed nitrogen comes from one source or another. For the health of your soil and the planet, however, you should practice organic fertilization techniques insofar as possible. As mentioned earlier, the scale of your farm may inhibit the cost-effectiveness of seeking organic certification. Especially in the early years of your efforts, you may need to apply chemical fertilizers just to get a crop, and this would rule out certification anyway. Using nonorganic plant food supplements carefully and in limited amounts will increase your yields dramatically. Meanwhile, work on building up the quality of your soil by the addition of compost, rock powders, blood and bone meals (unless you object to the use of these slaughterhouse byproducts), and wood ashes. Compost is the most important of these. Information on composting is provided in the Appendix.

In addition to providing the essential, major nutrients plants require, compost contributes to the soil's capacity to hold both air and water by supplying the "magic" ingredient, humus. Humus is a complex mixture of partially decomposed plant residues, such as the lignins that give wood its strength. Humus both absorbs water and entraps air bubbles, keeping these two essentials readily accessible to crop roots.

Compost and other organic fertilizers also contain varying amounts of minor and trace elements, such as magnesium and copper. Plants need these elements in relatively small amounts. Advocates of organic methods aver that because compost is made primarily of plant residues, all the necessary minor and trace elements are present in natural proportions.

Soils that receive compost, as opposed to a drenching with chemicals, also maintain healthy populations of beneficial microorganisms. Natural soils are a complex ecosystem in themselves, where bacteria, fungi, worms, and insects interact with each other and with plants. In a prairie or forest, when plants die their remains are recycled by this community of life. Nutrients gradually return to the soil in a form available to the next generation of plants. The teeming population of subterranean life also helps to keep harmful organisms at bay, so plants are less affected by pathogens and pests.

PHOTO BY JOHN TULLOCK

Beans sprout in soil amended with compost

Making compost from garden and kitchen wastes and then using it to grow food is the ultimate in household recycling. Organic fertilizer residues consist mostly of complex minerals and partially decomposed plant matter that break down over time and ultimately contribute to fertility. In other words, the soil becomes better able to sustain life.

Chemical fertilization has the opposite effect. Chemical fertilizers leave behind residual salts that, if left unchecked, eventually will make your soil unsuitable for crops.

Besides kitchen wastes, compost can also be made from other household trash, such as newsprint, cardboard, and office paper. Shredded, these components can be added to a compost pile or used as mulch. Few gardeners would disagree that composting creates a win-win for the gardener, the plants, and the environment.

Caution, Bacteria at Work

Despite the benefits of compost, be careful about incorporating organic matter directly into your growing beds. The initial decomposition of these materials can be counterproductive unless balanced with sufficient nitrogen to support the growth of beneficial bacteria. It is therefore best to produce compost in a separate pile or bin, then add it to the growing space. Unless you already have a supply of compost, rotted manure, blood meal, or some similar concentrated source of nitrogen, your plants will turn yellow and fail to grow when noncomposted material is applied directly to them. This is because the bacteria responsible for decomposition need nitrogen just as the crops do. The rapidly growing bacteria will out-compete your crops.

Chances are the soil in your yard has been abused long before you moved in. It will take several seasons to restore it, and in the interim you may be forced to add nitrogen from a bottle. Animal manures, traditionally the richest source of organic nitrogen, will likely be impractical if you are farming in a subdivision. Imagine the reaction of your neighbors if you have a dump truck load of fresh poultry manure delivered. If you make repeated additions of compost, use organic mulches, and allow the natural balance of the soil's

ecosystem to recover itself, fertility will rise. You will need less sup-
plemental nitrogen with each successive season and can eventually
dispense altogether with the bottled stuff.

Worm Your Way into Fertility

Chemical fertilizers will deter earthworms from inhabiting your
growing beds, another reason to avoid the bottle. The lowly earthworm is one of your best gardening friends, not only helping to
break down plant residues, but also by tunneling through the soil,
allowing the penetration of air and water. Earthworm "castings"
consisting of excreted soil particles and partially digested plant
matter is frequently sold as an organic fertilizer. Some specialty
growers swear by it. Each spadeful of soil from your vegetable patch
should contain a few earthworms. If not, adding more compost will
help attract earthworms during the growing season.

PHOTO BY JOHN TULLOCK

Greens in a raised bed

During the winter, inactive beds can be improved for the coming
season by inviting the earthworms in. Cover the growing bed with
black landscaping fabric, often sold as a weed blocker. This helps to
buffer the winter cold and provides shade, both features much beloved

by earthworms. The little holes in the fabric allow water to reach the soil below. Earthworms need moist soil. Scatter kitchen wastes, such as vegetable peelings, eggshells, and coffee grounds, on the surface of the bed. Incorporate them into the top two inches of soil with a hand spade, or sprinkle a thin layer of soil or mulch on top. This step helps prevent rodents or pets from investigating the bed. You can wait for earthworms to find the food, or you can add earthworms from a bait shop or perhaps from a friend's garden. Congratulations! You have just created an earthworm farm! The best time to do this is in fall, before the ground freezes. By spring, the bed should be teeming with worms, and ready to receive seeds or transplants of early vegetable crops.

Growing Green Manure

Cover-cropping involves following a harvest with a replanting designed to restore soil fertility. Cover crops are sometimes called "green manure." For example, after closing down your growing beds for the season, you might plant winter ryegrass or buckwheat as a cover crop. After they have produced a good stand of foliage, these quick-growing plants are tilled under to enrich the soil for the coming crop of vegetables. Legumes, such as clover, are frequently used as cover crops. They increase the nitrogen content of the soil even before being tilled under, because of the nitrogen-fixing bacteria associated with legume roots. Cover crops also shade out slower-growing weed seedlings, and extract plant nutrients from deep soil layers. Some even produce compounds that help prevent subsequent weed growth.

Planting by the Buddy System

Perhaps the best-known example of companion planting is the use of marigolds around the garden's border or between rows to help deter soil-borne nematode pests. Various other herbs and flowers can be employed in similar fashion. Lists of vegetables, herbs, edible flowers, and their recommended companions are presented as Tables 6-1 and 6-2. In some cases, these combinations deter pests, in others the companion attracts pollinators to the main crop. In some, experience has taught gardeners that the plants do well together, although the reason is unknown.

TABLE 6-1: VEGETABLE COMPANION PLANTING

Vegetable	Companions
asparagus	basil, calendula, parsley, tomato
bean	borage, brassicas, carrot, cucumber, eggplant, lovage, marigold, nasturtium, oregano, pea, potato, Swiss chard
beet	bean, brassicas, chive, garlic, lettuce, onion
brassicas	beet, chamomile, cucumber, dill, garlic, lettuce, mint, nasturtium, onion, potato, sage, spinach, Swiss chard, thyme
carrot	bean, chives, lettuce, onion, pea, pepper, rosemary, sage, thyme, tomato
cucumber	bean, brassicas, lettuce, marigold, parsley, tomato
eggplant	bean, marigold, pepper, thyme
lettuce	beet, brassicas, carrot, chive, dill, garlic, onion
melon	marigold, nasturtium, oregano, pumpkin, squash
onion	beet, brassicas, carrot, chamomile, dill, lettuce, pepper, Swiss chard, tomato
pea	bean, carrot, cucumber, mint, turnip
pepper	basil, carrot, eggplant, onion, tomato
potato	bean, brassicas, eggplant, marigold, pea
spinach	brassicas
squash	borage, marigold, nasturtium, oregano
tomato	asparagus, basil, bean, bee balm, borage, calendula, carrot, chives, cucumber, mint, onion, parsley, pea, pepper, sage, thyme, turnip

TABLE 6-2: HERB AND EDIBLE FLOWER COMPANION PLANTING

Plant	Companions
basil	pepper, tomato
bee balm	tomato
borage	bean, squash, tomato
calendula	asparagus, tomato
chamomile	brassicas, onion
chive	carrot, lettuce, tomato

TABLE 6-2: HERB AND EDIBLE FLOWER COMPANION PLANTING—*continued*	
Plant	**Companions**
dill	brassicas, lettuce, onion
garlic	beet, brassicas, lettuce
lovage	bean
marigold	bean, cucumber, egglant, melon, potato, squash
mint	brassicas, tomato
oregano	bean
parsley	asparagus, tomato
rosemary	bean, brassicas
sage	brassicas, carrot, tomato
thyme	brassicas, carrot, eggplant, tomato

By the same token, some plants do not grow well together. Often, the problem is that they compete for similar resources or attract the same pests. A brief list of some poor companions appears in Table 6-3.

TABLE 6-3: POOR PLANTING COMPANIONS	
Vegetable	**Avoid Planting Near**
bean	chive, garlic, leek, onion, shallot
beet	pole bean
brassicas	kohlrabi, nasturtium, pole bean, tomato
carrot	dill
cucumber	potato, sage
pea	chive, garlic, leek, onion, shallot
potato	cucumber, squash, tomato
tomato	dill, kohlrabi, potato

Practicing Integrated Pest Management

Integrated pest management (IPM) seeks to control or eliminate crop pests with a battery of techniques *other than* the application of chemical pesticides. IPM involves attacking pests on multiple fronts. Key IPM techniques take advantage of the pest's natural enemies and/or aspects of its life cycle to thwart its depredations on your crops. A simple example of IPM is burning, rather than composting, plant residues that might harbor pests through the winter.

Sometimes, physically preventing a pest from gaining access to your crops thwarts it. A deer fence is the most obvious example, or in a suburban setting, perhaps a fence designed to keep the neighbors' pets at bay. For insect pests, floating row cover, a fabric spun from plastic and so light in weight that it can be draped over tender young plants, provides several degrees of protection from frost damage and prevents access. Growing summer squash plants under row cover until the blooms appear is one way to foil the squash borer.

Other tools that can be employed in IPM include:

- Natural pesticides
- Nontoxic deterrents
- Trap-cropping
- Biological agents

Mother Nature's Pesticides

Pyrethrum and neem are among the more popular and widely available examples of natural pesticides. They are concentrated from the plants that produce them into commercially available forms that do the same thing in your garden that they did in nature: deter or kill insects that visit the plant to feed. Shaped by millennia of evolutionary adaptation, natural pesticides offer several advantages over their synthesized counterparts. Insects appear less able to develop resistance to these products, as they so often do with chemical agents.

Pyrethrum, obtained from a type of chrysanthemum, is a quick-acting poison that affects the insect's nervous system. Some forms of pyrethrum are not approved under organic production guidelines, primarily because they may contain synthetic compounds to enhance the effects.

Neem products contain extracts from an Asian tree species. Neem products are typically sold as a concentrate that is diluted with water before applying to plants. They act both to repel insects and to disrupt their growth cycles.

No Pests Beyond This Point

Nontoxic deterrents and pest traps can be highly effective. Snails and slugs damage a wide array of vegetable and nursery crops. Trapping them is one method of control. A widely circulated suggestion is to set out dishes of stale beer in the garden. Supposedly, slugs find the beer irresistible, become intoxicated, and fall into the dish and drown. It may be the result of their strict, teetotaling upbringing, but the slugs here in Tennessee don't seem to care much for beer. Coffee grounds, on the other hand, they adore. Thus enticed to gather in one spot, they can then be dispatched with commercially available poisoned baits sprinkled on top of the coffee grounds. Use bait containing relatively harmless iron phosphate, rather than the more common, highly toxic compound, methaldehyde. The latter is particularly dangerous for dogs, which are attracted to the pellets containing the poison.

Treatments for snails and slugs are always more effective when carried out just as the weather is warming in the spring. Three bouts of baiting spaced about two weeks apart keeps slugs and snails under reasonable control in my garden for the remainder of the season. I also kill them by hand, or more correctly by shoe, whenever I encounter them.

Putting up a snail and slug "fence" also works. Copper works as an effective barrier. To protect plants growing on benches, wrap several turns of uninsulated 12 gauge copper electrical wire around each of the bench legs. For raised wooden beds, you can staple two or three parallel rows of the same wire along the top of the bed frames. Copper sheet, cut into strips with tin snips, and attached to the bed frame with small nails also works. For beds in the ground, a fence of copper screen or flashing can be installed around the bed. It should be buried to a depth of four inches and extend above the soil surface by about the same amount. Burying the fence is necessary to prevent snails and slugs from crawling through the soil just beneath it. In all cases, the goal is to create a continuous barrier of copper enclosing the growing area. I have also used short lengths of copper pipe bent into a circle. These are placed around the base of each plant needing slug protection.

Another pest that may require control measures is the ubiquitous gray squirrel. Squirrels have become so accustomed to humans that they associate the human smell with food. Thus, if you bury something a squirrel may dig it up. That includes such things as onion sets and even the inedible bulbs of some types of nursery stock. Fortunately, a nontoxic squirrel deterrent is readily available: cayenne pepper. Purchase a large container from a restaurant supply house and liberally pepper the area when you plant bulbs or transplants. Marauding squirrels stop digging after one or two encounters with the hot pepper. You will need to replenish the cayenne after a rain. Eventually, the little gray thieves will associate your smell with sneezing and a burning sensation and forgo digging in your garden.

Sticky traps that attract flying insects to immobilization on glue-coated surfaces can be remarkably effective in some instances. Aphids, whitefly, fungus gnats, and cucumber beetles can all be controlled with them.

Using Crops as Decoys

Trap-cropping involves planting one crop that is sacrificed to pests, thus protecting the main crop. A good trap crop must be more attractive to the pest than the main crop. Trap crops can either be interplanted with the main crop or planted around it to create a living fence. The best method depends upon the crop being protected. For example, nasturtiums can be used to attract cabbage butterflies away from your cole crops. Flowering tobacco grown nearby can prevent aphids from attacking your tomatoes.

Making Biology Work for You

Using living organisms to control pests is frequently the most effective way of integrated pest management. Biological pest control agents include beneficial insects and microorganisms. For starters, eliminating pesticide use will help preserve the natural predators that may already inhabit your garden. Spiders, for example, prey on insects of all types, and their presence

PHOTO BY JOHN TULLOCK

Spiders prey on garden pests, such as the grasshopper

should be encouraged. I've even read reports of tree frogs being introduced into a greenhouse to control insects.

Various beneficial insects have been drafted for pest control duty. These include praying mantises, ladybugs, lacewings, and parasitic wasps. The several species of praying mantis are all predators that sit motionless, often near blossoms, to await the arrival of insect prey. Mantises do not discriminate in their choice of prey and will take beneficial species along with garden pests. Ironically, they are often the first insects wiped out by indiscriminate spraying because the mantis ingests pesticide each time it consumes another prey insect. Mantises can be introduced into your garden by purchasing the egg cases in fall and winter and attaching them to fences, shrubbery, or other areas about three feet above ground level. The baby mantises, as many as 200 per egg case, will hatch the following spring. With luck, the application of several cases will result in establishing a self-reproducing mantis population in your garden.

The mantis may be of minimal help in combating an overwhelming infestation by a single species of insect pest.

Perhaps the most widely used biological control insect is the ladybug. With over 350 species in North American alone, ladybugs, or lady beetles as they are sometimes more correctly called, have been recognized for centuries as beneficial to gardeners.

Ladybug adults hibernate, often gathering in great numbers to spend the winter protected from the harshest weather, and re-emerge in spring hungry for prey. They feed primarily upon aphids, but will also prey on various other insect pests. After building up their energy reserves through predation, they mate and lay numerous football-shaped eggs. The eggs hatch into larvae that eat other insects with the same voracity as their parents. Several generations can be produced before the onset of winter. Adult ladybugs can be purchased from commercial suppliers and released into your garden, or you can try attracting a natural population. Ladybugs like the flowers of members of the parsley family. Allowing parsley, carrots, cilantro, fennel, or dill to produce blooms in your garden helps to attract them. They are also attracted to some garden flowers, such as cosmos and scented geraniums. Late summer and early fall blooms should help bring in adults seeking pollen as a source of energy to store for hibernation.

Lacewings offer another option for biological pest control. Adult lacewings feed on nectar, pollen, and honeydew (the sweet excrement of aphids and some other insects). Their larvae are known as "aphid lions" in recognition of their insatiable appetite for the tiny, pesky aphid and a wide array of other small insect pests. If the garden is well planted with flowers to provide nectar for the adults, and if there are aphids around, lacewings may establish themselves. You can also purchase lacewing eggs to jumpstart the process.

Many wasps prey on other insects or their larvae, often as part of the wasp's own development cycle. Some wasps lay eggs in the eggs of other insects. Notable examples are the many species of *Trichogramma*, nearly microscopic killers of such pests as cabbage looper and corn earworm. You can purchase and release *Trichogramma* wasps into the garden to control a crop infestation. Other wasps parasitize the caterpillar stage. When I was a youngster growing up on a tobacco farm, the white cocoons of one such wasp regularly turned up on the back of tobacco hornworm caterpillars, looking like grains of rice. By that point, the caterpillar would be dead, reduced to an empty shell by the wasp larvae that had eaten it alive from within. This was my first introduction to the kill-or-be-killed ways of garden denizens. Wasp predation on other insects may be nonspecific. For example, the females of mud daubers and paper wasps typically sting a grub to paralyze it and place it in the egg chamber as living food for the wasp's offspring. Unless someone in your household is allergic to the stings, you should leave these predators unmolested. They are harmless unless provoked and will kill many of the insects that otherwise would feed on your plants.

The War Beneath Your Feet

Ordinary garden soil may not look like much, but to the ecologist it is a teeming jungle of interacting organisms. Not surprisingly, some soil organisms prey upon the insects that feed on our crops. Nematodes, tiny roundworms that live by the billions in soils worldwide, come in thousands of varieties. Several of these have been selected for their value as biological pest control agents, particularly for cucumber beetles, squash beetles, cutworms, and other insects with soil-dwelling larvae. Different species of nematodes are used to control different pests. Nematode products are simple to apply and target only specific insect pests. They are, like other organic controls, harmless to humans, pets, and other creatures.

WMD for the Garden

Bacteria that produce disease in certain insects have been employed in pest control for many years. Older issues of *Organic Gardening and Farming* often contained suggestions for "bug juice" remedies for garden pests. In general the advice was to collect a handful of the target pests, puree them in a blender with some water, and apply the resulting liquid to the infested plants. The idea was to increase the odds that naturally occurring pathogens would spread among the pest population. These crude preparations may have also been successful pesticides because they contain substances, such as hormones, that disrupt the life cycle of the pest insects.

One bacteriological control has been particularly well received. This is the bacterium *Bacillus thuringiensis*, better known as "Bt." Identified as an insect pathogen in the early 1900s, Bt was first used as a pesticide in 1920. The first commercial form, Sporine, appeared in 1938. Like Sporine, modern versions of Bt consist of the spores of the bacterium mixed with an inert carrier. The spores are extremely resistant, giving the product a long shelf life. By 1961, Bt was registered with the EPA as a pesticide. First observed in silkworm moths, and first used to control flour moths, the Bt strains initially available to growers were effective only against lepidopterous larvae, that is, the caterpillars of moths and butterflies. Growers of cabbage, broccoli, and cauliflower were among the first to adopt Bt for control of the cabbage butterfly, whose larvae feed on these cole crops.

Because Bt targets only specific insects, rapidly breaks down in the environment, and consists of natural bacterial spores, its use is considered entirely consistent with organic farming methods. Under the growing conditions available to me in Tennessee, organic production of cole crops would be impossible without Bt to control cabbage butterflies, for example.

Testing Your Soil

Without a soil test, it is impossible to know what soil amendments will provide the level of fertility necessary for crop production. For a nominal fee, you can have a soil test profile performed by your county agricultural extension agent. Be sure to check with the agency first to obtain directions for the collection and preparation of your sample.

For less than $20 you can also purchase a simple soil test kit at many garden centers. These kits work just like swimming pool tests. Put a sample of soil in a vial and add one or more chemical reagents. Comparing the resulting color with a chart gives you an estimate of the pH, nitrogen, phosphate, or potassium content of the sample.

Carrying out a soil test in fall allows you to plan appropriately to take steps to correct any deficiencies the test reveals. For example, adding agricultural limestone to correct the pH should be done prior to the growing season, allowing the lime about three months to have an effect. Similarly, mineral products such as greensand and rock phosphate need time to release nutrients, so you should apply them in fall. If the test reveals a need for nitrogen, a fall-planted cover crop may be just the ticket, since the crop will grow over the winter and be tilled under in early spring. On the other hand, it is probably not a good idea to add a chemical fertilizer or amendments such as wood ashes until shortly before planting time. Otherwise, rainfall will leach away nutrients before plants can absorb them.

Occasionally, a professionally done test will reveal that your soil lacks a trace element needed for production of certain crops. The element boron is needed by broccoli, for example. Broccoli deficient in boron develops a hollow, discolored stalk and pale flower heads. Insufficient calcium manifests itself as "blossom end rot" in otherwise healthy tomatoes. You may need professional assistance to identify and solve trace element problems. Remember that your agricultural extension agent is a great resource in this regard. The use of compost, rock powders, and other complex soil amendments greatly reduces the likelihood that deficiencies in trace elements will interfere with crop production.

Growing Vertically

A proper trellis is worth its weight in whatever vegetable it supports. By the same token, an unsatisfactory trellis may create more trouble than it saves. If you grow vegetables for market, you will increase your profits by investing in good trelliage. Growing crops vertically protects them from mud, increases the yield per square foot, encourages vegetables to form the most attractive fruits, permits

Peas on nylon trellis

increased air circulation (thus inhibiting many diseases), makes veggies easy to pick, and probably contributes other advantages that have not yet occurred to me! Thus, include these indispensable plant supports in your garden plan from the beginning.

Different crops require different types of trellises. Vines climb in more than one way. Peas, cucumbers, and melons climb via tendrils, specially modified leaves that curl around the support, anchoring the rest of the plant. Tendrils prefer to wrap themselves around supports about a quarter of an inch in diameter. In nature, these plants climb by clinging to small twigs. I find that wire fencing or nylon netting work best for these crops. Nylon trellis netting has openings about six inches square. The wire fencing has two-inch by three-inch openings. Either one of these trellises will support your plants, but I have found the nylon to be too fragile. Despite its much lower cost, nylon is not cost-effective; it usually only lasts a single season before it needs replacing. Wire trellis, especially if vinyl-coated, is significantly more durable. Neither one of these is suitable for all types of climbing crops.

Pole beans do not produce tendrils. Instead, their main stems twine around the support, and prefer a roughened surface about an inch in diameter. A wood or bamboo pole works best. Choose four poles about eight feet in length, and bury the ends about a foot in the ground, arranging them to create a "teepee," and planting two or three seeds in a hill at the base of each one. You can also use a single pole about three inches in diameter. Bury one end of the pole about a foot deep for each hill of beans, spacing the hills two feet apart. Plant four or five seeds in a circle around the base of the pole.

Designing a good tomato trellis poses different challenges. Tomatoes exhibit two growth forms, "determinate" and "indeterminate." The growth pattern is controlled by the tomato's DNA and cannot be changed by culture methods. In the case of determinate tomatoes, the size of the plant is limited to about four feet. (Some determinate varieties remain even smaller than this.) The plant grows to its predetermined size and stops. By contrast, indeterminate tomato plants get larger and larger as the season progresses. The stems keep lengthening as long as conditions conducive to their growth persist. Determinate tomato varieties bear a large crop of fruits all at once and thus are better suited to commercial growers who want to harvest a crop, sell it, and be done with it. Indeterminate tomatoes produce their fruits a few at a time, over a long season. For this reason, they are preferred by most home and specialty growers. Thus, the most useful varieties for your suburban microfarm's tomato crop will be indeterminate varieties. Consequently, you will need proper support for them in the form of a trellis.

I have been repeatedly led down the garden path, if you will pardon the pun, when it comes to tomato supports. I tried just about everything until I discovered the winning combination of pruning and trellising. This technique can increase productivity per square foot by several times that of plants left to sprawl.

The simplest support for tomatoes is a sturdy bamboo stake driven in the ground near the base of the plant. The stake should be taller than the anticipated height of the tomato vine at the end of the season, say six feet above ground level. The larger end of the stake, which should be about an inch in diameter, should be sunk at least a foot in the ground for stability. To prevent soil contact from rotting off the end, paint the stake with roofing tar or several coats of marine varnish, extending the protective finish about four inches above ground level. Periodically, you tie the tomato stem to the stake, choosing a point just above a node on the bamboo, which prevents the tie from

Tomatoes need sturdy support

slipping down. This alone would work great if tomatoes grew like Christmas trees, with a single leader and restrained side growth. But tomatoes are naturally rampant growers, sending out suckers from every leaf axil, and quickly creating a tangled mess, even when staked. Therefore, you should prune tomatoes to three main stems and use either multiple stakes, wire cages, or a wire mesh trellis to support them.

Trying to install a suitable trellis after the garden is already planted can be a challenge. Plan your crops and install trelliage at the beginning of the growing season. For maximum flexibility, I have built several raised beds with permanent trellising, allowing me to rotate crops among them. Because a well-built trellis system can last many years without replacement, it makes good business sense to do it right from the beginning. My system combines in one trellis suitable supports for both types of climbing vines, as well as tomatoes. The trellis is intended for attachment to the frame of a raised wooden bed, but you could modify it easily for installation directly in the ground. Use rot-resistant wood, such as cedar, cypress, or pressure-treated pine, for construction. My beds are all eight feet long, so I use four eight-foot lengths of two-by-four lumber to create a frame that is attached to the bed with long, exterior-use wood screws. I put uprights at each end of the bed, with a lower crossbar running between them about a foot above ground level. A second crossbar connects the uprights near their top ends. Six one-by-one-inch wooden poles are attached vertically to the crossbars. Spacing the poles at one-foot intervals creates the part of the trellis that pole beans can climb or to which tomatoes can be tied. To make the structure suitable also for tendril-climbers, I run lengths of galvanized wire horizontally, beginning just above the bottom crossbar and spacing them every six inches. The wires are secured to the small poles with fence staples, and to the uprights at each end via eye screws. Although this contraption will cost a bit, it will last for many years.

chapter seven

Get Fast Cash from Fresh Food

The quickest way to get into the market gardening business is to grow and sell vegetables. Demand for fresh produce remains high year round. Everyone needs to eat, of course, but there are other reasons for strong demand. For one thing, more and more people these days choose a healthier diet emphasizing fresh vegetables and fruits. A further advantage lies in the fact that vegetables are annuals, going from seed to harvest in a single growing season. Therefore, you can realize a profit from your vegetable farm during its first year of operation, if you are diligent.

In order to succeed in growing vegetables for market, you must have a good grasp of natural farming methods, a knack for organization, and a love of good food.

What Cooks Want

Irrespective of the species grown, vegetables must meet high standards if you expect people to buy them. Customers expect quality, variety, and a reasonable price. Every grocer knows we still judge food first by its appearance. I once tried to overcome buyer resistance with a sign reading "Cucumbers. Ugly, but Tasty!" for a basket of misshapen specimens. Not a single cucumber did we sell, and we ended up composting the whole lot.

Quality
Your first priority as a market grower should be to offer top-quality products. Vegetables grown to their best performance and harvested at the peak of ripeness should be your goal. Do not waste your time with varieties that don't perform well in your area—artichokes in the Deep South, for example, or okra in Maine. With proper arrangements you can grow almost anything anywhere, but the crop resulting from poorly adapted varieties is likely to be inferior. Your local cooperative extension service can provide a list of the best bets for your area. Find your local office at *www.csrees.usda.gov/Extension.*

Variety

Even if you grow only one crop, grow not only the varieties that you know to be popular with customers but also try offering some unusual ones that not everyone has seen. For example, most people are familiar with shiny red tomatoes, but not everyone knows about fuzzy yellow ones that look like peaches. Resist the temptation to move too far afield, though. Food preferences tend to be strongly cultural. If most of your customers have never seen a Chinese bitter melon, it won't matter much that yours are the best around. You can overcome customer resistance to new varieties by offering free samples and by sharing recipes. When planning your suburban microfarm, allocate only a small portion of your space to the varieties you hope to introduce. It is wisest to grow a small test crop the

PHOTO BY JOHN TULLOCK

Strive for quality and variety

first season. This permits you to determine if the market is ready for your innovation without having to make a large investment of money and effort.

Setting Prices

The best way to set prices at the farmers' market is to visit a large supermarket and note the current prices for comparable produce. For your fresh, local product you can add a premium to the supermarket price. For example, if you have naturally grown raspberries, you might charge 25 percent more than the grocery is asking for their imported ones. There is also no harm in charging the same price other vendors at the market are asking, even a little more if you think quality or some other factor justifies it. On the other hand, it is seldom wise to undercut your fellow vendors in the hope of improving sales. Not only will this earn you some ill will, but customer expectations may make it difficult to adjust prices later. Remember, you can always lower the price. Retail stores cut prices all the time. But an increase is difficult to pull off once you've stated a lower amount. One guideline I've encountered more than once is this: If only one or two customers per day complain, the price you've set is right. Of course, the ultimate test is whether you sell out by the end of the day. If not, perhaps your price is too high. If you sell out in the first hour, perhaps you should raise your prices next time.

Arriving at a wholesale price is another matter. A grocer or restaurant may feel justified in asking for a quantity discount off the regular retail price. I would caution against offering a discount to a chef without also offering others the same deal for the same volume of business. Keeping a secret in the food business is nearly impossible. Everyone talks shop with everyone else.

You can obtain price information for the largest wholesale vegetable markets online. Pricing for organic vegetables and livestock is published by the Economic Research Service of the USDA (see *www.ers.usda.gov/publications/vgs*).

Ethnic Cuisine

Growing vegetables that appeal to ethnic traditions can be rewarding. People who enjoy food enough to shop the farmers' market are likely to appreciate the special foodstuffs essential to the world's great cuisines. Even the most humdrum dish, like pasta sauce, can be rendered more authentically and deliciously Italian with ingredients such as "Genovese" basil, "Corno di Toro" peppers, and "Roma" tomatoes.

Consider grouping ingredients into baskets. The basil, peppers, and tomatoes might go into an Italian basket, perhaps with "Romano" green beans. A basket with a French accent might include fresh *herbes de Provence* (thyme, rosemary, sage, and oregano), tiny *haricots verts*, baby carrots, and a big bunch of sweet "French Breakfast" radishes. Florist and craft supply shops sell suitable baskets made from natural materials, as do produce brokers. Include a recipe or two with each basket, and make sure to provide the vegetables and herbs in amounts appropriate to the recipe. Enough food for either two or four servings per basket works best. You can even offer a credit for a returned basket. Why not? The customer returns to the market, you got another usable basket without spending any capital, and the basket is appropriately recycled.

Achieving High Productivity

A suburban microfarm by its nature has limited space. If you are going to reach a goal of $10,000 in annual sales, every bit of that space must be as productive as possible. Keys to achieving the most dollars per square foot include soil conditions, crop genetics, and market savvy. An integrated approach that takes into account each of these factors can maximize productivity.

Soil Conditions

Vegetables generally require higher levels of fertility than ornamental plants, particularly if performance is to be at maximum. In addition to providing nutrients, the soil controls access to vital moisture and air by the roots. The physical condition of the soil is called the "tilth." A loose, well-drained, friable mix of sand, organic material, and well-made compost will give the best results. Some crops, such as carrots, don't need rich soil so much as they need soil of homogeneous composition that does not restrict development of the roots. Time and money spent improving your soil will be repaid in productivity. If you strive for constant soil improvement, you will achieve good results with vegetable crops. Assuming, of course, that you also meet their needs for water and sunshine.

Crop Genetics

Some vegetable varieties lend themselves better to microfarming than others. Giants—for example, watermelon and pumpkins—

seldom pay you back for their profligacy in consuming space and nutrients. On the other hand, heirloom tomato cultivars, such as 'Cherokee Purple' and 'Mortgage Lifter,' taste so good and bear so well that they amply reward you for staking and pruning them, despite the availability of more compact types, such as 'Patio' and 'Celebrity.'

Many vegetable selections and hybrids have been bred for high productivity. Look for varieties intended for the home garden and those specifically targeted to farmers' market growers if you want plants that give abundant crops while remaining parsimonious users

Cucumber 'Marketmore 76'

of your space. The cucumber 'Marketmore 76' is a good example of a superproductive type developed for market growers. It yields a beautiful crop of uniform fruit over a long season, and does best when trellised.

Another benefit from the ceaseless activity of crop improvement is the development of temperature-tolerant cultivars that extend the growing season. Anything that prolongs the productive life of your microfarm will increase your profits. Judicious crop variety selection can lengthen the season by a month on either end. Look for cultivars intended for winter growing under plastic, for example. Conversely, heat-tolerant varieties can extend the season for cool weather crops that do not otherwise thrive in summer heat. Combining the right cultivar with appropriate culture methods can enable you to achieve almost year-round production, even in cold-climate areas.

Market Savvy

Understanding the value of a crop relative to the space it occupies requires observing the market price of various items in your area at different times of the year. When you shop, start making note of prices in the produce section, and create a spreadsheet tabulating your observations. Soon, patterns will emerge. You will probably discover, for example, that having a crop available a mere two weeks on either side of the main season can increase the price of an item by 50 to 100 percent. You will also be able to calculate an average retail price per unit for the season during which you can bring in a crop. Knowing this and the crop yield per square foot allows you to calculate the productivity of that crop in dollars per square foot.

With this information you should be able to allocate space easily, first placing the most productive crop, followed by the second most productive one, and so forth, until you run out of either room or crops. Keep records of productivity for everything you grow each year so you can refine your projections. You can use published estimates of crop productivity (see Appendix) as a starting point, but because productivity is highly dependent on local conditions, it is best to rely on data developed for your area— or better yet, on your own records.

The Crop Plan

A crop plan is a representation of your microfarm over a single growing season. Creating a crop plan enables you to anticipate the inputs of materials and labor that will be required to turn a profit. Developing a crop plan requires you to take numerous factors into account. Because of the variety of vegetable crops that can typically be produced in a single location during the course of a season, the plan for a vegetable garden is the most complicated one you are likely to encounter. Thus, creating a vegetable crop plan provides good training for the development of a plan for any other type of crop.

The elements of the crop plan are:

- Species and cultivars you intend to plant
- Number of individual transplants or feet of row to be sown for each variety
- Anticipated planting and harvest dates for each variety
- Notation of succession planting to maximize space utilization
- Anticipated yield for each variety

It is helpful to note how you plan to sell the crop, especially if you expect to use several different marketing methods.

chapter eight

What Vegetable Crops Should I Grow?

In order to decide what vegetables to grow for market, you must consider both productivity and ease of culture in your area. Following is a summary of basic information on commonly grown vegetables. You should also locate information specific to your region of the country. The best way to do this is via your state's cooperative extension service (see *www.csrees.usda.gov/Extension*).

Artichoke

The delicious flower buds of this giant thistle can command high prices at the market, but unfortunately the artichoke does not thrive in many parts of the country. A recently introduced variety, 'Imperial Star,' that matures a crop in one year may offer hope to growers unable to bring the standard plants through winter. Besides being difficult, artichokes take up a lot of space, at least a square yard per plant, in order to yield about six flower buds. I recommend including them in your repertoire only if you have a lot of room and prior experience growing them successfully. Most of the artichokes sold in the United States are grown within a few miles of Castroville, California, where they luxuriate in Pacific fogs and moderate temperatures.

Asparagus

Another perennial, asparagus has been enjoyed since ancient times. It is a member of the lily family and therefore a relative of the onion. Like other members of the onion clan, asparagus likes rich soil and dislikes competition from weeds. It takes at least two years, and usually three, to get an asparagus patch ready for production. However, once established, the same bed can yield a crop every spring for decades. Driving country roads, I sometimes see feathery fronds marking the site of an old planting, still going strong long after abandonment. If you have room for a bed of asparagus, purchase plants, rather than starting from seed. This saves a year of waiting and avoids the hassle of dealing with the delicate seedlings. Most authorities recommend planting asparagus in trenches, spaced to allow you to walk between them. Add two or three inches of well-made compost to the bottom of the trench. Avoid harvesting any shoots the first season after transplanting, and take only a few the second. Thereafter, you should get a decent crop each spring. After harvest, side dress the plants with plenty of compost and keep them irrigated during dry spells. Mulch with straw, wood chips, or pine needles, and promptly remove any weeds that come up through the mulch. The best asparagus grows in a weed-free environment. Despite the high retail value for a pound of asparagus, you should only go to the trouble if doing so won't be taking up space that could otherwise be planted with a less-demanding crop.

Basil

Although technically an herb, basil must be grown as an annual in most of the country because of its utter intolerance of cold. Therefore, it lends itself to inclusion in the vegetable garden alongside tomatoes and peppers, two of its best culinary partners. Basil is started from seed and transplanted to its permanent location after all danger of frost has passed and the ground is well warmed. It will bear continuously until the first light frost touches the leaves. Dried basil loses much of the appeal of the fresh herb, with the result that fresh basil is in good demand year round. Greenhouse growers, take note that out-of-season basil is typically the most valuable product per pound that you might produce. To harvest, pick the most succulent tip growth from mature plants. Each of these cuttings should be about six to eight inches long, with at least two pairs of large, mature leaves below the top crown of smaller ones. Bunch the cuttings in sixes and tie with raffia. Immerse the stems in a vase of water almost up to the lowermost leaves. *Do not refrigerate.* Cold will turn the leaves black. When you reach the market, protect the bunches from the sun to prevent wilting. To have a regular supply, you will need at least a dozen basil plants. Basil cuttings root quickly. Take them from your early crop and root in water. Transplant the cuttings into the garden when the roots are about two inches long, and keep well watered until the plants resume growth. Pick off all flowers and flower buds from basil plants to prolong their productive life. Keep the plants well watered and side dress every two weeks

Basil 'Mammoth'

with compost or another organic fertilizer.

Numerous basil varieties are available. For general culinary purposes, choose a large-leafed type. 'Mammoth' bears huge leaves big enough to use for wrapping pieces of food for steaming. Lemon, lime, and licorice-scented basils are available. Also include in your product mix Thai basil, which smells a bit like teaberry, and basils with colorful foliage, such as 'Purple Ruffles.' All are grown in the same way.

Beans

Almost any reasonable soil will produce a good crop of beans, and just about any bean is worth growing. Virtually all the beans produced for farmers' markets are snap beans.

The market value of beans, as you will quickly learn, is related to the difficulty in picking them. It can be a tedious, backbreaking task. That is the main reason market growers of my acquaintance prefer pole beans. These also produce slightly more pounds per square foot than bush beans do. If you prefer to grow bush beans, however, they will sell equally well.

A particular bean variety may be highly esteemed in your area. Heirloom beans with names like 'Greasy Back' and 'Pop's Peanut' are some of the most sought-after types in my region. No doubt your neighbors have their favorites as well. Since heirlooms seldom, if ever, appear in conventional supermarkets, customers will seek them out at the farmers' market.

Green beans come in many cultivars, ranging from tiny pods the diameter of a pencil to big, flat Italian versions half an inch wide and nearly a foot in length. There are waxy yellow ones and bright purple ones. The former cook quickly and have a smooth texture. The latter turn green when cooked, but they are easier to see when picking. Among the hottest sellers are the French types known as *haricots verts*. These are not merely immature pods of other bean types but rather have been bred specifically for "baby" bean production. Available in both bush and pole types, they are a bit more finicky than regular green beans but can command a 50 percent price premium if you grow them well. Wait until the dew has dried, pick carefully, and only sell perfect, whole beans with a short bit of stem still attached. Unlike other green beans, which are best displayed in bulk, haricots will suffer from handling by customers if dumped out in a pile. Instead, display them in baskets or small bunches tied with raffia, and watch them disappear.

Plant beans in mid to late spring when the soil temperature has reached sixty degrees and all danger of frost is past. For support, nothing beats a bamboo or rough-sawn one-by-one-inch wooden pole sunk firmly into the ground and at least eight feet tall. The poles should be about eighteen inches apart. Plant four or five seeds around the base of each pole.

Beets

Beets enjoy a small but devoted following. Like other root crops, beets need only modest amounts of nitrogen but benefit from soil rich in phosphorus. Individual beet "seeds" are actually fruits containing multiple seeds. Thinning, therefore, is always a must. Incorporate the leaves of the removed seedlings into salad mixes, where they will contribute both flavor and color. Your other salad crops should be ready to harvest at about the same time you are thinning the beets. Gourmet cooks prefer baby beets about the size of a golf ball for salad dishes, and more mature ones, tennis-ball size, for classic dishes such as borscht and red flannel hash. Try providing recipes for beet dishes to improve your sales.

Harvest beets when they have colored up properly and are the size you want. Overgrown specimens are woody and worthless, so it is best to err on the side of early harvest. Sell them by the bunch. Three or four is enough if they are mature. Baby beets should be bunched in dozens or half-dozens. Beet tops are also edible. Swiss chard is a beet variety cultivated specifically for its tops and succulent stems. Grow it the same as beets. For both, cool weather during the growing season results in top quality. Your plantings must be timed appropriately if you live in a warm summer area.

Consider growing some of the interesting varieties of beets and Swiss chard, such as the beet cultivar 'Chioggia.' It has concentric rings of red pigment alternating with white, visible in a target pattern when the roots are cut crosswise. The chard cultivar 'Bright Lights' produces stems in white, yellow, pink, and purple, topped with dark green leaves. Including these brightly colored veggies in your product mix will help your display stand out. Both beets and chard are well worth growing because they command a good retail price and produce about a pound per square foot.

Broccoli

Brassicas, or cole crops, include the various members of the cabbage family. One of the most nutritious is broccoli. Broccoli heads, which are actually the flowers, must mature while the weather is cool or else quality suffers. Timing is therefore essential to success. For warm summer areas, it is best as a fall crop. In the Deep South, you can grow broccoli as a winter vegetable. In cool summer areas, produce two crops per year. Each plant requires about four square feet of fertile soil, and they can be a bit persnickety. If the plants suffer stress at any point from seed to flower, the yield and quality of the crop is likely to be severely impaired. Do not allow seedlings to become stunted. Transplant to the garden about sixty days before you expect to harvest, and side dress when they are a foot tall. A well-grown crop will usually return a profit because of high demand. Broccoli has been touted as a "super" food because of its many health benefits. These, along with its flavor, no doubt contribute to its popularity.

Brussels Sprouts

A cool-season crop like Brussels sprouts that allows multiple pickings seems designed for the market farmer. In most of the United States, this brassica should be grown as a fall crop. Warm weather when the sprouts are maturing will make them bitter and unsalable. The plants will even tolerate a light frost. Some growers maintain that this actually improves the flavor. Start seed for transplants five weeks before you plan to set them out. The plants should go into the garden about ninety days before the anticipated first frost. The sprouts are formed in the leaf axils (the point at which the leaf stem attaches to the main stalk) and develop from the bottom of the plant upward. Harvest when the sprouts are approximately an inch in diameter.

Cabbage

From sauerkraut to *kim chee*, people all over the world eat *Brassica oleracea*, European cabbage and its related species. Heat-tolerant cultivars of cabbage exist, but generally speaking it is a cool-weather plant. Compared to its relatives, broccoli and cauliflower, cabbage is easy to grow. The plants must receive protection from snails and slugs, the cabbage butterfly, and drought, but otherwise they present few difficulties. Cabbage requires fertile and well-aerated soil. As with many other crops, raised beds work best and allow you the closest spacing. Each plant should be allocated four square feet. Cabbage holds well in storage and therefore is usually inexpensive in grocery stores. Growing red cabbage or Savoy cabbage, a variety with extremely wrinkled, frilly leaves, may prove to be a wiser move than offering your customers standard coleslaw.

Carrots

A friend once asked me, "Why grow carrots, when they are so cheap at the store?" I answered his question by offering him a bite of a freshly pulled homegrown carrot. He was immediately convinced. Good carrots will grow in comparatively little space with minimally fertile soil. They appreciate phosphorus, as do all root crops. Do not overfertilize. Too much nitrogen severely impairs quality, producing forked roots. A loose, sandy soil at least six inches deeper than the longest anticipated mature roots should be your goal. Full-size, foot-long carrots will be difficult to achieve if you don't have really deep soil. Instead, choose varieties that produce short, fat roots, such as 'Thumbelina.' Also grow cultivars that yield true baby carrots, which have good color and taste when only two or three inches long and half an inch in diameter.

PHOTO BY JOHN TULLOCK

Carrot 'Little Finger'

Supermarkets seldom offer genuine baby carrots. Rather, they sell plastic bags containing pieces of larger carrots whittled down by machine to resemble the genuine article. Yuck! Cultivars such as 'Little Finger' and 'Bambino' produce perfect baby carrots with luxuriant tops, even under trying circumstances.

Besides the usual orange ones in various sizes and shapes, there are purple and yellow carrot cultivars. Give them a try. Being such a familiar and versatile vegetable, carrots that think outside the box will attract customers wanting something different. Rinse freshly pulled carrots well, trying not to wet down the tops. The goal is to remove as much soil as possible without rubbing, which can damage the root's delicate skin. Remove foreign matter from the tops, and any dead or yellowing leaves. Bunch them by the dozen or half dozen and tie with raffia. Store carrots cool and in high humidity, but avoid letting them lie in water. Keep most of your stock in a cooler and only display as many bunches as you expect to sell in an hour. Wilted carrots turn customers off. Mist the display of carrots now and then to keep them looking shiny and bright orange. Take along one or more spray bottles filled with cold tap water. Misting also helps to keep other produce spruced up while on display.

Cauliflower

Another close relative of cabbage, cauliflower often presents challenges outside cool summer regions. In the hot, humid South or the arid Southwest, bringing in a decent crop of cauliflower will require some climate-control measures and may thus not be worth attempting, despite the high retail price commanded by a luscious snowy white head. Everything said about growing broccoli applies to cauliflower. When well grown, cauliflower will yield a higher return per square foot than broccoli will. To achieve a perfect, white head, some cultivars must have the outer leaves tied up around the developing flower bud. Other, "self-blanching" varieties don't require this extra labor, and therefore generate more profit.

Chervil

An annual herb that should be treated as a vegetable for market purposes, chervil peps up food with a licorice note not unlike that of tarragon, only milder. It is delicate in appearance but easily grown in cool, moist conditions. Because it does not dry well, fresh chervil will be snapped up by eager cooks. Grow it in spring or fall if summers are hot where you live. Culture is similar to that for parsley.

Cilantro

Another annual herb that lends itself to cultivation in the vegetable garden, cilantro grows best when the weather is cool but will tolerate considerable warmth. For quickest germination, soak the seeds in water overnight before broadcasting where the plants will grow. Cilantro does not like to be transplanted. Make successive plantings a week apart in order to have a continuous supply. Cilantro should be pulled up by the roots rather than being cut. Wash off the soil, but try not to wet the foliage, as this reduces its keeping qualities. Remove immature or damaged plants from the bunch, tie loosely with raffia, and refrigerate on a layer of damp paper towels in a closed container.

Corn

The first sweet corn announces with certainty the arrival of summer. Despite its undeniable popularity with consumers, however, fresh sweet corn offers little to the small-scale farmer. Corn is enormously greedy. It requires copious supplies of nitrogen, water, and sunshine, and then most plants only produce one or two ears. Heirloom varieties tend to be even less productive than the modern, super-sweet hybrids. As a rule, each plant needs a square yard of growing space, but you will be doing well to earn a dollar an ear at the market. That translates to about a quarter per square foot for your efforts. Grow sweet corn for your family if you enjoy it. You might even sell a few ears if you can bear to part with them, but you probably cannot grow sweet corn profitably without plenty of extra space.

Cucumber

If ever a vegetable were designed with the needs of the market farmer in mind, it would be the cucumber. The vines produce loads of luscious fruits over a long season, and dozens of selections and hybrids can be culled to find the best fit for your growing conditions. Growing cucumbers on a trellis not only saves space but also results in nearly perfect fruits because they hang from the vines, forced by gravity to grow long and straight. Some cucumber cultivars are intended primarily for pickling, yielding a heavy crop of small, slightly curved fruits. While pickling cucumbers can certainly be eaten fresh, the relatively short harvest season is a drawback. If you have some extra room for cucumbers, however, you can test your customers' preferences for the pickling types. Succession planting allows more than one crop per season, because cucumbers only take about sixty-five days to mature. They must have rich soil, an inch of water per week, and good air circulation.

Dill

A summer annual herb, dill is welcomed near the end of the season when it is traditionally used in making pickles. Its flowers attract beneficial insects, making dill another herb that should be treated like a vegetable. You can preserve cucumbers, okra, beans, and even green tomatoes by pickling. The distinctive flavor of dill enhances all these products. Grow dill alongside okra, as the two have similar requirements. Some dill varieties produce both usable foliage and seeds. Other varieties have been bred to produce mostly foliage with few seeds. The latter will be more esteemed by cooks looking for fresh dill, which is used to enliven fish and potato dishes, among others. Dill seed heads are more commonly used for seasoning pickles.

MAKING CANNED PICKLES AND RELISHES

Pickles and relishes are not only easy to make, they offer the perfect way to create a value-added product to enhance your microfarm income. Canned products can extend your selling season long after the growing season has passed. Start with time-tested recipes, such as the one below, then develop your own.

Because pickles and relishes are highly acidic, they resist spoilage. Nevertheless, all require processing under boiling water. Pints and half-pints, the most profitable sizes, require ten to fifteen minutes of processing, timed from the point at which the water returns to a rolling boil. Use distilled white vinegar of five percent acidity (sometimes labeled "50 grains" of acidity) and do not dilute except as specified in the recipe. Use noniodized salt labeled for making pickles.

The beauty in making pickled green tomatoes is that you create a profitable use for those undersized, unripened tomatoes at the end of the season. And few recipes are simpler to prepare. Use fruits one to one and a half inches in diameter. They should be as hard as a baseball, with no trace of ripening. If you have misshapen ones, trim off the unsightly parts.

PAY DIRT PICKLED GREEN TOMATOES
10 pounds green tomatoes
7 cups vinegar
7 cups water
½ cup salt
Garlic cloves, peeled and left whole
Dill seed
Whole bay leaves

Wash the tomatoes, core them, and cut them into halves or quarters. The resulting pieces should be more or less uniform in size. Pack them into hot pint jars. To each jar add 1 garlic clove, 2 teaspoons of dill seeds, and a bay leaf.

Combine the water, vinegar, and salt in a saucepan. Bring to a boil and pour over the tomatoes, leaving ¼ inch of head space. Wipe the rim of each jar carefully and apply the lid. Process the jars for 15 minutes in a boiling water bath. Carefully remove the jars, using jar tongs made for the purpose, and allow them to cool to room temperature. Store in a cool, dark place.

Eggplant

The colorful, versatile eggplant thrives on summer heat and produces a crop comparable to tomatoes, though less abundant. The eggplant makes a tidier plant than the tomato, seldom requiring more than one stake for support and needing little in the way of pruning. It is not as easy to grow as tomatoes, however. If started too early, eggplant can be devastated by flea beetles when it is stressed by cold. The leaves of young plants become perforated with pinholes from the depredations of the tiny insect. Growing seedlings more than thirty-six inches above ground level deters the pests, because the bugs apparently won't fly above this altitude. Flea beetle control is essential for a marketable crop, as plants seldom reach either their productivity potential or best flavor after an infestation. Besides the large, purple Italian ones seen in supermarkets, eggplant comes in pink, white, lavender, and striped varieties, as well as in elongated, hot-dog shapes and nearly spherical forms. The tiny sweet fruits of cultivars specially developed for "baby" eggplant production are popular with customers at my local farmers' market.

Endives

Belgian endive and radicchio are botanically the same plant, chicory. Both are grown for winter forcing to produce the edible shoots. During the growing season, all effort is directed toward developing the healthiest plants possible. In the case of Belgian endive, the roots are dug and stored in fall for forcing during the winter. In the case of radicchio, the plants are cut to the ground in fall, and resprouting produces the reddish-purple, bitterly tasty heads. Either crop is worthwhile if you are willing to expend the effort. You can bring endive roots out of storage and force them as needed, making it the more logical choice for a small operation. The plants are easy to grow, requiring only adequate room and reasonable care. The downside for either is that the market is not as large as for annual greens such as lettuce.

Garlic

Garlic has adapted through centuries of cultivation to nearly every place on Earth habitable by humans. Fall-planted cloves will mature a crop the following year, but for the largest, best-quality bulbs the plants can be left in the ground to grow for a second season. In either case, remove the flowers as soon as they appear. Like onions, garlic thrives best in rich, weed-free soil. Given this and sufficient water, bringing in a crop is easy. The bulbs can be grown more closely spaced than onion bulbs.

Kohlrabi

This brassica is another of the seemingly endless variations on cabbage. Grown for the swollen stems that form at ground level beneath a rosette of cabbagey-looking leaves, kohlrabi has a savory, nutlike flavor. It is grown like cabbage, and the information given for that vegetable applies. It may be attacked by cabbage butterflies, and is susceptible to slug damage. This is a good crop to try if you want to introduce something different at the farmers' market.

Leeks

Yet another member of the onion family, leeks prefer a long growing season of cool, moist weather. In a suitably mild climate, they provide a good crop to grow over winter, when little else is occupying the garden. For the market grower with limited space, leeks present the same difficulties as other members of the onion family—a need for plenty of nutrients, the absence of competition, and a long season of growth. With these factors provided, however, you can produce a leek crop worth more than a dollar a plant at retail. Baby leeks, which can be thinnings removed from the bed when they are about twice the diameter of a pencil, can also be sold profitably. Start leeks from seed, and transplant when they are six inches tall, spacing them about six inches apart. Subsequently remove every other one for baby leeks. Harvest the remainder when they reach an inch in diameter.

Lettuce

For the market grower, lettuce can be the mainstay of the early and late seasons almost anywhere in the country, and an all-season producer where summers are cool. The best lettuce matures when temperatures remain between 50 and 70 degrees Fahrenheit over the course of the day. With good technique, you can bring in a lettuce crop within six weeks of sowing. Thinnings can be sold as baby lettuce, often commanding a bit more per pound than the mature product.

Hundreds of lettuce varieties exist. Most growers agree that your best bet is to grow several types for a salad mix. Cultivars adapted to specific growing conditions abound. There are summer lettuces, for example, that tolerate much more heat than other types. Many heirloom varieties can also be found in catalogs. You may even be able to identify local favorites.

PHOTO BY JOHN TULLOCK

Lettuce 'Oakleaf'

Lettuce seeds can be broadcast directly in the growing bed or you can start them in cell trays. Only the latter approach should be used when you want perfect, uniform heads. Use broadcast sowing for "cut and come again" harvesting. Cutting the leaves with scissors and allowing the plants to sprout again from the roots gives you at least two crops from a single planting. The downside is a reduction in plant vigor, and the harvest becomes more perishable.

The small plants produced by thinning can be sold as baby lettuce, but pulling them is tedious. It also increases the amount of soil you must clean from the harvest, because soil clings to the roots. Few customers want unwashed lettuce. The object of thinning, of course, is to allow the best plants to grow to maturity with plenty of room. If this is your main goal, forgo the potential sales of baby lettuce and start seeds in cell trays. Fill a thirty-six-cell tray with seed starting mix, water well, and make a small indentation in the surface of the planting mix with a blunt object, such as the eraser end of a pencil. Drop two or three seeds into each indentation. Lettuce needs light to germinate. Do not cover the seeds, but water gently from the top to settle them in. Placed under artificial lights or in a greenhouse, at 70 degrees the seeds often germinate within twenty-four hours. They are ready to transplant to the garden in about two weeks, when plants have two or three sets of leaves and roots are just beginning to appear in the drain holes of the cells.

Leave four to six inches between plants in each direction. Water the transplants, and side dress with compost. Feed them every two weeks. Plan on harvesting lettuce about a month after transplanting. Stagger plantings in order to have lettuce maturing every week until the weather becomes too hot. Heat causes lettuce to turn bitter and bolt, or go to seed. Romaine and Batavian lettuces are among the most heat-tolerant varieties, but even these peter out in the blistering heat of August here in the upper South. For the warm climate grower, lettuce can be produced as a winter crop, and it performs well under cover where just a few degrees of frost protection are required. Well adapted to greenhouse cultivation, too, lettuce can be a staple for any grower.

Lettuce can be started on a sunny windowsill

Melons

These sweet, luscious relatives of the cucumber always find a ready market, but they take up a lot of room for the number of fruits produced. Experiment with unusual varieties, and grow them on a strong trellis. You will need to support the developing fruits with cloth slings secured to the trellis. One taste of a melon cultivar such as 'Charentais,' however, will confirm the effort is worth it. Look for local favorites that may be specially adapted to your region. Plant breeders have developed cultivars with short vines that consume less space than traditional ones. Some varieties, such as watermelon, get much too large for a trellis, and probably will not sell for enough money to compensate you for the trouble of growing them.

Miscellaneous Greens

Many other greens besides lettuce have found their way onto American plates over the past two decades. Arugula, to name one, has been famously associated with upscale dining since President Obama campaigned in Iowa. Other examples of "exotic" salad greens include dandelion, mache, mizuna, purslane, sorrel, and tat-soi. All of them can be grown alongside lettuce, performing best during cool weather. Quality suffers when the weather heats up.

Bane of suburban lawns, the dandelion was originally a salad green or potherb, and made its way to America as seeds packed in the luggage of European colonists. Like its relative, lettuce, it escaped from cultivation and has become a weed. However, the leaves of cultivated dandelions make a delicious addition to salads, and it poses no threat to the rest of your garden because for top quality it should be harvested long before flowers are produced. Look for "domesticated" dandelion cultivars in specialty seed catalogs.

Mache is a delicately flavored green that tolerates cold so well that it can be planted in fall and left to overwinter. Also called corn salad, lamb's lettuce, and rapunzel, it is always eaten fresh. Grow as you would lettuce, but cover the large seeds to a depth of about one-half inch. Thin to stand about two inches apart. The thinned seedlings can be transplanted or sold as baby greens.

Mizuna is an Asian mustard that offers the distinct advantage of multiple harvests from a single planting. The tartly flavored, ragged leaves can be cut three or more times. It grows in any reasonable garden soil during cool weather, and will be ready a mere three to four weeks from sowing. Flea beetles can be a problem when the weather is too warm and dry, rendering the leaves unsalable. Grow under a floating row cover and keep well irrigated to foil the tiny pests.

Purslane is unusual among salad greens in having succulent leaves. It also contains significant amounts of omega-3 fatty acids. With news reports on the value of omega-3s in promoting circulatory system health, look for purslane to enjoy increasing demand. Considered a weed by many, purslane is extremely easy to grow. Scatter seeds where you want the plants to grow, or start in flats and transplant to the garden in early spring.

Sorrel provides another example of a plant widely considered a weed but esteemed by gourmet cooks. Unlike other greens, it is perennial, but it warm summer areas suffers miserably if water is not abundantly supplied. Establish the plant in rich, moist, well-drained soil. Even where summers are warm, if properly tended it will bear harvests for several years without replanting. Sorrel adds its lemony flavor to soups as well as salad mixes.

Tatsoi is botanically the same species as mizuna. Sometimes called spoon lettuce, tatsoi produces large rosettes of deep green leaves. Tolerant of cold and shading, it should be grown as described for mizuna.

Okra

Okra, also known in the South as "gumbo," is an annual hibiscus that loves heat and humidity. Seeds will rot in cool soil, so wait until the ground has warmed thoroughly and the weather is stable before you plant. Soak seeds overnight to hasten their germination and sow about an inch deep in any reasonably fertile garden soil. Some growers like to plant okra seed in hills and thin out all but the strongest plant. Okra also transplants well and can be started in cell trays. Space transplants about twelve inches apart for "dwarf" varieties and twice that for the larger heirloom types. You should have pods ready to harvest about six weeks from transplanting. Okra must be harvested daily, removing every pod. The best quality pods are about three inches in length, although some cultivars can be allowed to grow longer without their becoming too tough.

Leaving stray pods on the plant reduces the overall yield, and the pods

PHOTO BY JOHN TULLOCK

Okra 'Dwarf Long Pod'

themselves become woody and inedible. Wait until the dew is off the plants to pick, and do not wash the harvest. Store the pods in a perforated vegetable container under refrigeration for a maximum of three days. If the pods begin to turn dark, use them immediately, as you will not be able to sell them.

Okra plants are covered with short bristles that will irritate your skin. Wear long sleeves and gloves when you harvest. Even the supposedly nonirritating 'Clemson Spineless' cultivar leaves me itching. Okra will yield more than a pound of pods per square foot, and sells for the same price as green beans, owing to the labor involved in harvesting. These factors make it worthwhile to grow it for market.

Onions

Just about everyone loves these pungent members of the lily family, from scallions to sweet Vidalias. In the garden, they thrive on rich, moist, well-drained soil. They do not tolerate weeds, the presence of which will reduce the crop yield. Onions come in many forms, adapted to varying growing situations.

Scallions are discussed later in a separate section. Bulb-forming onions include both long-day and short-day types. In these, the timing of bulb formation is controlled by the length of the day. If you try to grow short-day onions in the spring, you won't get onions. They must be fall planted. Certain varieties of fall-planted onions produce the unusually sweet bulbs that Vidalia, Georgia, is famous for. Low sulfur content in the soil around Vidalia accounts for the special flavor of the trademark onions, but sweet onions can be produced anywhere with a sufficiently mild winter and long, warm spring season. Sweet onions are planted in fall for harvest around June. Long-day onions are planted in early spring, to produce bulbs during the extended days of summer. They are typically grown from sets, tiny bulbs that give rise to larger onions after several months, and are harvested in early fall. Their bulbs contain less sugar and thus typically fare better in storage than sweet onions do.

Shallots are grown like garlic, with fall planted sets maturing almost a year later. Shallots can be trickier to grow than other members of the onion family, but they also command a higher price at the market.

For the microfarmer, the surprisingly little-known perennial onions may be your best bet. Once a bed is established, perennial onions will deliver a crop with minimal attention. Two types of perennials exist. Egyptian, or "walking," onions produce shallot-like bulbs as "topsets." These are little bulbs appearing at the tip of a long, upright stalk where you'd otherwise expect flowers. When the topsets enlarge enough, their weight causes the stalk to bend over, and they plant themselves a short distance from their parent. In this manner, they "walk" all over the place unless you restrain them. That's easily done, simply by removing any offenders, which can be used like shallots.

The other perennial onion is sometimes called a "mother," "multiplier," or "potato" onion. Each bulb divides during the growing season to produce several more. By separating and replanting the bulbs, you establish a patch that will produce all the onions you care to dig. Select some to sell or eat, and replant the rest.

Parsley

Another herb, parsley is best treated as a vegetable crop, like lettuce. Because it is biennial, parsley will overwinter in mild areas, providing both late and early crops from the same fall planted patch. With careful succession planting, you can have parsley available any time. Cooks prefer Italian, or flat leaf, parsley for seasoning, and the curly varieties for garnishing platters.

Parsnip

Seemingly the carrot's less fortunate cousin, the parsnip never gets the attention it deserves. It takes much longer to produce a crop than is the case with carrots, rendering parsnips twice as expensive as carrots and consequently less popular in the marketplace. I suggest growing a test crop before you devote a lot of space to them.

Peas

Like beans and other legumes, peas are not difficult to grow. Their retail price largely reflects the labor involved in picking them. Few crops, with the possible exception of sweet corn, are so eagerly awaited each year. Bring in a good crop of peas, and you're likely to sell out at the market every week.

Peas come in two forms, edible-pod forms and those with tough, fibrous pods. The latter are frequently called "English" peas. They must be shelled before use, although the pods can be added to soups that are pureed and strained before consumption. Fresh shelling peas are becoming ever more scarce in the marketplace. The effort to grow them requires their retail price to be equivalent to that of the edible-pod types. Yet, about half the weight is shells. Although frozen peas have taken over the market, devotees of early peas may be willing to pay the price for your fresh ones. A test crop will help you determine if growing them is worthwhile.

Edible-pod peas are another matter. They can be eaten straight from the vine, are attractive on the plate, and taste as sweet as candy. Also known as snow or sugar peas, they are the microfarmer's friend. The only drawback is the necessity for daily picking to ensure highest quality. Pay attention to seed development within the pods. These pea varieties lose quality rapidly when the outlines of individual peas can be seen. Pick them much earlier than this, while the pods remain flat.

One of the greatest advances in vegetable crop development resulted in the snap pea. This vegetable combines the best features of both pea types, producing edible, sweet pods that retain quality even when the seeds start to mature. Over-inflated pods can be shelled. The pods will have become too tough to eat, but the peas will be just fine. 'Sugar Snap,' the first of these cultivars to be marketed to home gardeners, needs a sturdy trellis, as the vines easily reach eight feet. Pods are produced over a long season.

All peas resent hot weather, which results in rapid decline of crop quality. In hot summer areas you can grow any type of peas for fall harvest, in addition to producing a spring crop.

Peppers

Peppers bear so abundantly, it is hard to imagine a better warm season cash crop. Growing good peppers is relatively easy in soil of average fertility. The biggest problem may be misshapen fruits resulting from stressful growing conditions. Provide an inch of water weekly, especially where summers are hot.

Start peppers in pots and transplant when the ground has warmed up. They dislike cool soil, uneven moisture, and excessive fertility. Moderation in all things, except sun, seems to be the key. Sweet bell peppers yield the largest fruits by weight and are number one in popularity with consumers, but you will find a ready market for banana peppers, both sweet and hot, chilies in their numerous incarnations, and specialty peppers such as the fiercely hot habanero. Because peppers can be used at all stages from immature to fully ripe, they provide a crop over a long season. In hot summer areas, bell peppers will slow down, then rebound and produce a fall crop if you keep them fed and watered. Keep all peppers free of weeds and thin the fruits mercilessly. Leave the perfect specimens to ripen if you want the best quality, and sell the smaller ones. Keep the misshapen specimens for your own use. Pepper plants are highly decorative, with their glossy green leaves and brilliantly colored ripening fruits. For this reason, they are an ideal choice for integrating into the suburban landscape.

Potatoes

Unlike most other vegetables, potatoes prefer acidic soil. They also require ample room. The space demanded by potatoes, about four square feet per plant, yielding about five to eight pounds of mature potatoes, may render them too greedy for your purposes. Nevertheless, if you can provide the room, specialty potatoes sell for top dollar. Potatoes originated in the New World tropics in ancient times, and have proven themselves so genetically malleable that the number of varieties almost defies tabulation. From the huge russets we normally think of as "baking" potatoes, to tiny gems the size and shape of baby cucumbers, potatoes offer something for every palate and nearly every grower. Don't bother trying to compete with the pros by growing supermarket varieties. Choose instead local favorites and heirloom types that originated in conditions similar to yours. There are potatoes with colorful flesh in red, yellow and blue, along with various skin colors, shapes, and starch levels. Suppliers sometimes offer sample packs of only a pound or two of seed potatoes. This provides an excellent means to test multiple cultivars. In my area, the soil in many places is naturally acidic. As a result, some potato varieties perform extremely well. The most popular cultivars for my region are 'Kennebec,' 'Red Pontiac,' and 'Yukon Gold,' but I've had good success with 'All Blue' and a yellow-fleshed fingerling type, too. Growers in cooler climates will have more cultivar choices. In the Deep South, potatoes make a fine winter crop.

Radish

If you don't count indoor crops like alfalfa sprouts, nothing matures as quickly as the radish. Another ideal choice for growing in limited space, radishes can be succession planted for multiple crops throughout the cool part of the season. They demand only loose, well-drained soil of average fertility. Look for varieties in red, white, and purple, and combine them in one bunch for a patriotic theme. (A true blue radish is not available.) The cultivar 'Easter Egg' produces variously colored roots from a single sowing. Old reliable types like 'Champion' should not be overlooked for producing a classic round, red radish. For sweetness in a larger root, try 'French Breakfast,' which produces a pink and white, watermelon-shaped root about an inch and a half in length. Offer samples to your customers with a pinch of sea salt, and they will sell themselves. Do not overlook long white radishes such as "Icicle."

PHOTO BY JOHN TULLOCK

Radish 'French Breakfast'

Rhubarb

Another in the "grow if you have the room" category, rhubarb is a true perennial. It is grown from root cuttings. Like asparagus, it requires establishment in rich, fertile, well-drained soil for a couple of seasons before you can begin to harvest the juicy stems. High oxalic acid content renders the leaves inedible. Rhubarb has its fans, and the plants are quite decorative in summer. But the market is small and the harvest period rather brief.

Scallions

Green onions are so mundane, they are often overlooked by market growers. Bunches of crisp scallions, freshly pulled with their roots still on, sell well when displayed alongside other spring delights, arranged in neatly tied bunches at $1 apiece. Tie them around the roots and again around the tops, to keep the plants from curving due to their attempts to grow while in storage. Unlike other onions, scallions never form a large, rounded bulb, and may be direct seeded in succession all season long, though quality is highest in cooler weather. Like other members of the huge onion clan, scallions need rich soil and the absence of weeds to yield well. Harvest them when the largest leaves are about the diameter of a pencil.

Spinach

As a salad green, young, tender spinach lends its buttery goodness to mixes, or stands on its own. Blanched or steamed, spinach not only provides an abundance of minerals and vitamins but also adds a subtle, elegant flavor to savory dishes from quiche to quesadillas. Related to beets, spinach can be direct seeded as early in spring as the soil can be worked. It tolerates frost well, and matures a crop in about two months from sowing. It will produce about a half pound per square foot. For the finest quality, thin spinach to a spacing of three inches each way when the plants are about four inches tall. The plants removed by thinning can be sold as baby spinach. Wash them, spin dry, and present them in plastic bags holding about four ounces. Mature spinach should be pulled up, roots and all, washed free of soil, spun dry, and sold in bunches tied with raffia. This preserves the quality longer. The stems are eaten as a vegetable, separately from the luscious leaves, in some cuisines. Popeye was right about the nutrition packed into spinach. All those minerals come from the soil, of course, indicating that spinach needs high fertility in order to yield a good crop.

Squashes

Squashes come in two basic types, summer and winter. The former bear earlier, have thin skins, and don't keep very well, while the latter mature late, have thick skins, and keep for months. Both types need plenty of space and have numerous insect enemies, but they bear heavily on sturdy plants that do not require trellising. Look for "bush" varieties intended to maximize space utilization. All squash types are heavy feeders. Further, they should not be allowed to dry out to the point of wilting the leaves. Thus, they demand a lot in return for their bounteous harvest. In some areas of the country, insect pests, such as the squash bug and squash borer, severely limit productivity unless the plants are kept covered until blooms develop. Check with your local extension agent or find out from other gardeners the control measures required in your region. Squash is a New World native, and so are many of its pests. The squash borer, for example, is the larva of a moth found throughout much of North America. This explains why the bugs can be so persistent and destructive.

Summer squash 'Dwarf Bush Scallop'

If you conquer its enemies, squash will reward you with abundant fruit. Three pounds per square foot is not unreasonable to expect. Pick them when young, making sure to remove all fruits. This will keep the plants producing over the longest possible season. Squash flowers are a splendid delicacy. Some cultivars have been developed solely for flower production. They must be picked daily, as soon as the blooms open. They can be stored for no more than two or three days. Squash blossoms are obviously a pain to harvest, but if your customers are food savvy they should snap them up and beg for more. I suggest offering six for $5. Provide recipes if you want to test market squash blossoms.

Sweet Potatoes

Another space hog, the sweet potato yields over a pound per square foot in warm climates. Typically, you begin with slips, small plants started for you by a commercial grower. Growing your own will require a greenhouse, because they must be started early. The slips are planted in hills, two or three plants to the hill, the individual hills occupying about four square feet. With plenty of water and fertilizer, the vines will run all over the place, and each hill should produce about five pounds of roots. Where sweet potatoes grow well, you'll find numerous varieties including local favorites. Once again, my advice is to grow them only if you have room left over after accommodating more valuable crops.

Tomatoes

King of the summer garden, the tomato provides the market grow-er's best opportunity for profit. Nearly everyone loves vine–ripened tomatoes, and they grow well all over the United States. Seek out heirloom cultivars, try some of the many hybrids available, and grow as wide a variety of tomatoes as you can. Stagger plantings to maximize your harvest period, giving preference to the indeter-minate types. Properly staked and cared for, they will be the most productive plants in your garden.

I've grown dozens of tomato cultivars over the years, from local heirlooms like 'Cherokee Purple' to modern hybrids like 'Celebrity.' The heirlooms are by far the most satisfying to grow, and their flavors are outstanding. Heirloom tomatoes typically are regionally adapted, so you will need to do some research to find the best ones for your location. Many claims regarding soil types and culture techniques are made by rival growers, but my experience suggests genetics plays the largest role in taste.

Growing good tomatoes poses few challenges to a capable gardener. Tomatoes do, without exception, need staking and pruning in order to be maximally productive. (Pruning was mentioned in the section on trellising in Chapter 6. See the detailed information on tomato pruning in the Appendix.) They are subject to a host of diseases and conditions, all of which can be controlled to some degree by good culture technique. For example, uneven watering causes fruit to split in hot weather, sharply reducing productivity. Use soil-level irrigation and apply a deep mulch. Mulch also helps prevent soil from splattering the lower leaves, which usually leads to fungal infections. I prefer a natural mulch, such as pine needles, but many gardeners swear by plastic sheeting. The latter helps warm the soil, allowing a somewhat earlier planting than otherwise. Black plastic is most often used to optimize the heating effect, but red plastic has been shown to increase productivity, probably because it reflects the red wavelengths, which would be absorbed by black plastic. Red light is beneficial because chlorophyll evolved to absorb red light.

PHOTO BY JOHN TULLOCK

Tomatoes should be started in cell trays and transplanted to the garden when they are about six inches tall or larger. They are easy to carry along in pots, so you can have plants ready to go into the ground just about any time you want if you plan well. If plants in cells start to get overgrown, just pot them up into a gallon container. When

An abundant harvest of tomato 'Sprite'

you are ready to plant a leggy, container-grown tomato, remove all but the top one-third of the leaves and bury the plant almost up to the lowermost set of remaining leaves. Water daily for the first week to encourage the establishment of a strong root system, then switch to normal irrigation.

Harvest tomatoes while they remain firm, or even with green shoulders. While there's no harm in bringing to market a few tomatoes that are ready to eat that day, their fragility increases dramatically when perfectly vine-ripened, so beware of harvesting too late. Also, bear in mind that your customers may visit the market only once a week and will want tomatoes that will keep for a few days, achieving optimum flavor on the kitchen counter. Your best bet is to offer fruits in varying stages of ripeness. Green tomatoes as hard as a baseball are preferred for frying.

Turnips

Another "second tier" crop, turnips yield both roots and tops, thriving in cool weather. While many people enjoy turnips, they do not sell in great quantity and thus should be included in your crop plan once other, more valuable crops have been allocated space. Turnips grow like radishes, to which they are closely related, but need more space to develop their tennis-ball-size roots. Some turnip cultivars have purple shoulders on the roots, while others produce a pure white crop. Plants removed by thinning can be used for cooked greens. Indeed, cultivars are available intended for production of tops alone. Try test marketing baby turnips in your area. Plucked when the roots are the size of a golf ball, they are steamed or poached whole to the delight of gourmet cooks.

Thinking Like a Chef

I once heard a chef say to his students, "Knowing how to cook will get you a job, but understanding food presentation will get you promoted." This advice applies equally to the farmer who wishes to sell produce. How you prepare and display your offerings can mean the difference between merely selling and selling for top dollar.

Start by emphasizing quality in every aspect of growing the plants. Vegetables need coddling. Accordingly, you should spare no effort to grow perfect specimens. Any produce that does not look attractive should be used in your kitchen, not offered to your customers. Insect damage and other defects should be absolutely minimal in the harvest you take to market.

Follow proper storage procedures for all harvested crops. Greens, for example, need rapid cooling to counter field heat, or quality will suffer. Given that it is unlikely you will pick everything on market day, you must arrange to store early pickings properly. Some things need refrigeration, others keep best at room temperature. (Links to information on crop storage can be found in the Appendix.) It makes little sense to invest the money and effort required to bring in a fine crop, only to reduce its salability through improper storage.

The need for cleanliness cannot be overstated. No one wants to get dirty hands while shopping for vegetables. Gently, carefully, and thoroughly clean everything. Washing can be destructive to some crops—for example, okra. Instead, use a small brush to remove any dirt from the pods. Carrots, on the other hand, will keep better if the roots are rinsed well under cold water prior to storage. Make sure to drain them thoroughly, and minimize the amount of water remaining on the tops, which promotes mold growth. Even though the leafy tops of root vegetables might not be eaten, their appearance matters. Remove yellowed, damaged or broken leaves from beets, kohlrabi, radishes, and turnips. If you plan on holding the crop more than a couple of days prior to market, remove the tops about an inch above the crown and store only the roots themselves. Refrigerate in a sealed container.

Most summer vegetables should be gently wiped with a cloth after picking. Tomatoes, in particular, should never be washed or refrigerated. Green beans should be kept cool, but handled as little as possible to maintain the best appearance. Washing will lead to mold growth and spoilage.

On the other hand, wash all greens in at least two changes of cold water. Fill a sink, dump in the freshly harvested greens, and let them sit for a few minutes to allow soil to sink. Scoop them out with your hands, avoiding any floating debris or yellowed leaves. Keep your fingers spread, using your hand like a garden fork, to capture the greens and leave debris behind. With practice, you can rinse a sinkful in less than a minute. Repeat the process at least one more time. Then spin dry in a salad spinner, prior to storage in perforated plastic bags under refrigeration. Properly washed greens will keep longer and in better condition than unwashed ones.

As a general rule, care in harvest and the use of mulches will keep all but root crops from getting too dirty. This will render post-harvest cleaning much less of a chore.

The Package Sells the Product

Packaging is important. Ask anyone who designs products for retail sale. The ideal package not only protects and displays the product, but also looks attractive enough to encourage the customer to add the product to his or her shopping basket. Use raffia, for example, rather than rubber bands, to tie up bunches of radishes, carrots, or scallions. Observe the techniques used by fancy food shops to entice customers, and imitate them. Containers made from natural materials look more inviting than plastic ones, so use wooden crates, reed or wicker baskets, and rough cloth sacks. Cushion easily bruised produce with shredded wood or pine needles. Try different arrangements, and take a digital snapshot of each one. Ask your family and friends to evaluate your ideas. Ask yourself if you would be tempted to buy.

chapter nine

Find Herbal Remedies for Your Budget

Were herbs to disappear, dining would be a humdrum affair. Herbs, herbal products, and herb gardening have become ever more popular over the past few decades. Cut fresh herbs command hefty per-pound prices, herb plants pack garden centers each spring, and natural herbal products may outnumber their synthetic counterparts on the shelves of some stores. From the grower's standpoint, herbs have much to recommend them. Most are adaptable, easy to grow, and attractive in the landscape.

Besides the perennial culinary herbs, numerous species are grown for their fragrance and/or medicinal value. Including a variety of herbs in your crop plan is a good idea, therefore, whether they are to be your main focus or simply an adjunct to the vegetable garden.

In this chapter, I've included only the perennial culinary herbs. The culinary annuals are best treated like vegetables by the market grower, and are therefore covered in Chapter 8. Herbs that are not typically used in the kitchen are also covered in the present chapter, as are edible flowers, which, like culinary herbs, can be used to enhance both visual appeal and taste. Fruits, which bring their unique flavor notes to both sweet and savory dishes, are also discussed here for the sake of convenience. All these plants can add to the bottom line of any suburban microfarm. They also offer the added benefits of wide-ranging adaptability, high-dollar productivity, and beauty in the residential landscape.

PHOTO BY JOHN TULLOCK

The author's herb garden

Perennial Culinary Herbs

The beauty of growing perennial herbs for market is that you can obtain multiple crops per year. Most herb varieties have been selected for their ability to withstand repeated pruning and bounce back within a few weeks. They also take up relatively little room and can be tucked here and there in the landscape. Herbs also typically root easily from cuttings, allowing you to produce numerous offspring from a few stock plants in a relatively short time. Incorporating herbs into the garden can have other benefits, too. For example, garlic chives and lavender deter Japanese beetles and can be located close to plants that the beetles frequently attack, such as okra or roses. At the end of the season, you can prepare numerous value-added products, from potpourri to soap, that feature herbs. Foodstuffs of any kind require the use of a kitchen inspected by the local health department, but you can create and sell nonfood herbal products without restriction.

Bay

Perennial in the subtropics, bay laurel survives outdoors to Zone 6 with protection. (Find your hardiness zone at *www.usna.usda.gov/Hardzone/ushzmap.html.*) It can also be grown in a large container and brought indoors for the winter. The glossy, bright green leaves are indispensable in many cuisines, notably Italian and Creole. Under good conditions, a bay tree can grow larger than twelve feet in height but can be maintained indefinitely at a manageable size by judicious pruning. Container plants will also need root pruning every two or three years. Buy established plants and don't remove any leaves the first year. Wait until the tree is taller than two feet before you harvest or prune. Keep the soil constantly moist, but never soggy or the roots will rot. Mulch plants growing in the ground with a few shovels of compost each spring. Container plants can be watered monthly with an organic fertilizer, such as compost tea. Seed-grown bay varies in the quality of its flavor. Choose stock plants whose leaves smell really good, and propagate your own additional plants by taking stem cuttings when your trees are large enough. Take cuttings in early autumn, which is also a good time to prune. If you have room for several trees, you can make laurel wreaths for holiday sales from the abundance of prunings. Stressed trees are likely to attract spider mites, but bay is generally free of pests and disease.

Chives

Like its relatives in the onion family, the chive is among the easiest and most productive of savory plants. Easily started from fresh seed, chive plants that have matured into a foot-wide clump can be divided to yield dozens of offspring. Chives grow best in well-drained, humusy soil of average fertility. They do not require heavy feeding, as onions do. They also tolerate partial shade better than other members of the family. Cut chives about two inches above the ground when the plants are at least six inches tall. Don't cut when the leaves are wet, as the keeping time will be greatly reduced. Chive flowers, which should be picked in early morning as soon as they are open, make a tasty garnish. Cut the stem at ground level. Be sure to remove every flower you find. This will encourage a second bloom later in the season. Chives do not dry well, so freshly cut or living plants are in demand.

Chives, Chinese

Chinese chives are also known as "garlic chives." They do indeed taste more like garlic than like onions. They will grow vigorously on any soil of average fertility, and besides providing savory leaves for cutting all season produce lovely, edible white flowers in umbels at the top of two foot stems. They do have a tendency to self-sow all over the place, but this is easily remedied by removing the flower heads before the seeds mature from bright green to black. Once established, the plants will thrive without further attention. Mine grow happily amid other perennial flowers. Some gardeners blanch the plants, either by piling mulch around the emerging leaves or by wrapping the clumps in newspaper jackets, to produce yellow chives. The blanching results in a milder flavor. You can let a few flower heads go to seed, then pot up seedlings to offer your gardening customers. Be sure to mention that they repel Japanese beetles if these pests are a problem in your area.

Lemon Balm

Lemony-flavored herbs abound, and the refreshing citrus touch appears in dishes from every cuisine. Lemon balm is one of them. It is considered a weed in many localities because it self-sows. Unlike other members of the mint family, however, it does not produce invasive runners, but instead forms a neat, rounded mound about one to two feet tall and the same diameter. The bright green, toothed leaves have prominent veins. Start from seed in spring, or take cuttings anytime during the growing season. Seedlings can vary in flavor. If you have established plants with a flavor you like, dispense with seeds and use only cuttings for propagation. Although mostly used for tea, lemon balm can be incorporated into any dish where a lemon flavor is desired. The flowers can also be used as a garnish, or included in bouquets. Grow it in full sun, unless you live south of Zone 7, where afternoon shade is best. Stressed plants will get powdery mildew, which does not seem to reduce their vigor, but renders the leaves useless. Therefore, keep them well watered, and allow space between plants to permit air circulation.

Lemongrass

Essential to Thai, Vietnamese, and other Asian cuisines, and a good source of lemon flavor, lemongrass is a tropical perennial that must be wintered indoors or started anew each season. Because it needs a large container for its prodigious root system, starting over each year is the best technique outside the frost-free regions of the country. In my view, it is not sufficiently ornamental to warrant the trouble of growing it as a houseplant. I usually visit the local Asian grocery in early spring to buy new starts. Lemongrass is sold in bunches of several stems with most of the foliage removed. Each stem has a bulbous base. When planted, the bulb roots and quickly grows into a clump a yard or more in height and about as wide. Insert the stem about an inch into a small pot of damp soil mix, and roots will quickly form. You may even see tiny roots or root buds sticking from the base of the bulb. When new roots protrude from the drain hole in the pot, you are ready to transplant outside, but wait until all danger of frost has passed and the weather is warm. Stand back! If sited in full sun and rich, moist soil, lemongrass grows with amazing rapidity. As you might expect, the vigorous growth comes with demands for plenty of nutrients and water. Container plants should be fertilized regularly to keep them producing. In the garden, add compost to the bottom of the planting hole, or side dress monthly.

The leaves of lemongrass have sharp, serrated edges that can deliver a nasty cut. Wear heavy gloves and a long-sleeved shirt when working with them. Remove foliage with clippers, and trim to eight or ten inches in length. Offer three to five stems to a bunch. The stem base should be about half an inch in diameter. Lemongrass often takes on a reddish cast, enhancing its decorative value in the landscape. You could even use it as a protective, although temporary, hedge.

Lemon Verbena

A subtropical perennial, lemon verbena wins my vote for the best lemon-scented herb. Combining the essence of lemon with a pleasant floral undertone, it is the perfect herb for a refreshing tea, or to flavor a syrup for drizzling on fruit. References restrict its range to Zones 9 and 10, but the plant grows with protection at least as far north as my Zone 6 garden, and adapts readily to container culture.

When grown in the ground it forms a mound about three feet in diameter. The stems bear glossy, medium green, serrated leaves in whorls. The tiny, edible flowers, white or pale purple in color, appear in late summer. Cuttings can be taken any time during the growing season and will be ready to transplant the same year if started early. Harvest the leaves by cutting lengths of stem just before you go to market. Keep the cut ends in water, as the plant wilts readily. If the plant gets rangy looking because of all the pruning, cut back mercilessly to six inches above the base and allow new sprouts to develop.

When the first frost turns the leaves brown, cut to the ground and cover with an inverted flower pot or small bucket to help keep the crown from getting sodden. Atop the cover, pile up a mound of leaves or mulch to protect the roots over winter. As the ground warms in spring, carefully check for the emergence of new shoots. I start looking around the frost date. When growth is evident, remove the mulch and the cover to give the plant unfettered access to sun and air. You can also take cuttings late in the season to provide next year's crop. After rooting, winter the cuttings indoors in one-gallon nursery pots. A sunny window or a bank of fluorescent lights will keep the plant going until you can move it outside once more. If you grow multiple plants in a bed, keep them separated by three feet or more to prevent their hungry roots from competing. Like all tropical herbs, lemon verbena is a heavy feeder.

Even the woody older stems carry the delightful fragrance. Cut pruned stems into six-inch lengths and bundle them with raffia. Offer the bundles to the gourmet cooks among your customers, with a suggestion to use them for smoking fish on the grill. Thin stems can also be used as flavor-imparting skewers for grilled foods.

PHOTO BY JOHN TULLOCK

Lemon verbena

Lovage

Lovage is a perennial member of the carrot family that looks and tastes a lot like celery. The plants can reach six feet in height, so plan your landscape accordingly. It prefers cool conditions and partial shade, but will grow in sun where the weather remains cool. Definitely not a plant for the warmer regions, lovage can be started from seed or by making divisions of a mature plant. The seeds, produced from abundant umbels of lacy white flowers, also carry the celery flavor.

Marjoram

The flavor of marjoram is similar to, but sweeter than, its cousin oregano, and it works in the same dishes. A tropical perennial, marjoram is grown as an annual in most of the country. It prefers well-drained soil of average fertility, and reacts poorly to overwatering. Start seeds in four-inch pots in spring, and transplant to the garden after all danger of frost has passed. Successive plantings will allow you to cut bunches for sale all season. Marjoram turns bitter after flowering, so be sure to harvest before flowers form. Side dress the plant with compost after each pruning. Do not use chemical fertilizers, or even concentrated organics like fish emulsion, as too much nitrogen will result in an altered flavor.

Mints

Invasive to a fault, these perennials will quickly take over a bed, crowding out everything else. All the culinary mints form clumps about two feet in diameter, with taller spikes of summer flowers in pink, lavender, or white. The blooms attract many insects that will pollinate your other crops. Mint will grow in any soil and in sun or shade, but for the best quality, grow them in light shade with abundant moisture and starved for nitrogen. Fertilizing will result in rampant, leggy plants with small leaves and harsh flavor. Mint seeds do not necessarily produce offspring with the same flavor as the parents, but they are a cinch to root from cuttings. Plants from cuttings will have the same flavor as those from which the cuttings were taken. Just buy a bunch of fresh mint at the grocery, recut the stems, strip all but the topmost leaves, and set them in a glass of water. Place the glass near a sunny window. You'll have rooted plants in three weeks or less. Choose your propagation stock by taste and appearance. You can also buy started plants from a nursery, but taste a leaf first, as these are likely to be seedlings. Mint holds up well when fresh cut, and dries well, too. You can also offer started plants. Due to its invasive habits, mint is a good choice for containers, where it can be kept in bounds. Even a large container planting lasts only a season before the plants become bedraggled from their confinement. Toss them and start over next year. The most popular mint is probably peppermint. Other good choices include spearmint, apple mint, and pineapple mint. All are grown in the same way. Although not used as an herb, Corsican mint, with tiny, rounded leaves, is a good ground cover for dish gardens and thrives in cool, moist semi-shade.

Oregano

Oregano is another member of the mint family. It is better behaved than its just-discussed cousins but can become invasive where the soil is too rich. It is a spreading, trailing plant with woody stems a foot or two in length and fuzzy, rounded leaves. Like other members of the family, oregano seedlings vary greatly in their flavor. Cuttings root easily, and once you have a few plants you

PHOTO BY JOHN TULLOCK

Greek oregano

can produce more any time you want them. If you grow oregano from seed you will observe that some plants have white flowers while in others the flowers are pink. Most references describe the pink-flowered forms to be of inferior flavor, making it necessary to cull ruthlessly. Your best guide to quality, however, is the taste. Sample any prospective stock plants before you buy. Full sun and good drainage are necessary to grow good oregano. It makes a superior dried herb if cut just before flowering. For a container garden, oregano is the perfect trailing plant to adorn and soften the edges of the pot. Customers will want cut oregano in bunches of six or eight stems, and the live plants in small pots.

Rosemary

I associate rosemary with roast chicken, a near perfect culinary match in my view. This is another subtropical plant that can be grown far outside Zones 8, 9, and 10, with a little protection and judicious selection of cultivars. The strain known as 'Arp' is widely grown here in Zone 6. Among its many desirable qualities, rosemary adapts easily to training. Pink or blue flowers, depending upon the cultivar, appear in earliest spring, and are edible. As with many other herbs, rosemary seedlings vary considerably. Your best approach is to buy plants propagated from named cultivars. Otherwise, you have no idea what to expect. Softwood cuttings taken in early summer root easily and allow you to expand your stock. You will need multiple plants to provide many cuttings for sale in bunches or as potted starts. Space them well apart, keep lightly moist but never wet, and fertilize with a side dressing of compost in early spring. Overwatering will encourage fungal diseases to attack the leaves, while a thorough drying-out will set the plant back for the remainder of the season. Don't try to grow rosemary if you cannot give it full sun. Not only will the plant be weak, it will also not have much flavor. Some rosemary cultivars, such as 'Barbecue,' produce an abundance of long, straight stems you can cut at eight to ten inches in length. Suggest to customers that they strip the leaves from the lower end of these stems. The leaves can be chopped for seasoning and the remaining stems used as skewers for grilling, where they will impart their flavor to the food.

ROSEMARY-INFUSED MASSAGE OIL

If you make food products intended for human consumption, health regulations will require that you do so in a properly licensed kitchen. In all likelihood, you will not be able to obtain a license for your family kitchen. Thus, you may be forced to add a second kitchen to your house, or to find a commercial kitchen to rent. Either way, the cost can be significant.

However, products that are labeled "Not for Human Consumption" usually do not come under the purview of the Health Department, and you can prepare them at home for sale at your favorite venue.

Making herbal massage oil is a good way to turn a garden surplus into greenbacks. Use "pomace" olive oil for these products. It is produced by extracting the residual oil from already pressed olives, and commands a price far lower than either "extra-virgin" or "pure" olive oils. The aroma is also very weak and thus won't compete with your herbal additions.

For oils, sterilize bottles by placing them in a 250°F oven for twenty minutes. Turn off the oven and allow the bottles to cool with the door closed until they are cool enough to handle before you fill them. *Never add cool liquid to a hot glass container.*

PAY DIRT HERBAL MASSAGE OIL

6 cups rosemary leaves, stripped from the stems
6 cups pomace olive oil

Set a large metal bowl over a saucepan or stockpot filled with simmering water. Adjust the heat so that steam escapes around the bowl. When the bowl is hot, add the rosemary leaves, pour the oil over them, and allow to infuse for twenty minutes. Remove the bowl from the heat, allow to cool, and carefully strain the oil into sterilized bottles. Cap, label and store.

Sage

Like so many other members of the mint family, sage is best propagated by taking cuttings of named cultivars rather than sowing seeds. Perennial to Zone 4, sages unfortunately are short lived and will require periodic replacement. Do this when the plants start looking bedraggled, usually after three or four years in the garden. Take softwood cuttings in spring, and transplant to the garden when roots are well formed. Offer bunches of cut sage along with potted plants to your customers. Many sage varieties are more ornamental than culinary in their uses; some have a downright unpleasant flavor. As with other herbs, tasting a bite will tell you more than any amount of reading. The purely ornamental sages are long lasting in arrangements and when dried can be used for making wreaths.

Tarragon

Although perennial in Zones 4 to 8, French tarragon languishes in the heat and humidity of summers in the Sunbelt. There it will perform halfheartedly, if at all, only with protection from afternoon sun. Where summers are cool and humidity is low, however, it thrives in full sun and fertile, well-drained soil. French tarragon does not produce seed. Buy plants that have been propagated from cuttings. Once you have established some plants, increase your supply by taking cuttings in fall, just before they enter dormancy. You'll need to overwinter the cuttings indoors, then transplant to the garden in spring. Alternatively, new plants can be obtained by dividing a mature specimen in early spring, at the same time you would divide perennial flowers.

The rich, anise-like flavor of French tarragon has no precise substitute, but Mexican tarragon comes close. If you live in a warm climate, Mexican tarragon will prove far easier to grow. It is perennial and roots easily from cuttings, but is not frost-hardy. As a bonus, Mexican tarragon produces bright yellow, edible flowers.

Thyme

Were I to grow only one herb, it would be thyme. Not only does thyme add a subtle, savory note to countless dishes, its various species and cultivars create one of the most ornamental assortments of herbs one might assemble. Basic culinary thyme includes numerous cultivars with variegated leaves, and even one ('Orange Blossom') that smells faintly of oranges. Most cooks will want French thyme, a variety that produces long, unbranched stems from which the tiny, gray-green leaves can be quickly and easily stripped. Another popular variety is lemon thyme. In addition to the culinary forms, there are numerous species and cultivars used primarily for ornament. One of my favorites is 'Elfin.' Deep pink flowers cover the plant in midsummer. It joins several other thymes as a good choice for "living grout." Thymes like lime, which explains why they do so well when grown between concrete pavers or intermixed in paths of limestone gravel. Besides the need for lime, thymes require full sun, but they demand little else from the gardener. They react negatively to too much of either water or fertilizer. If you grow thyme to sell as a cut herb, expect to replace the plants every two or three years, as they become woody and bedraggled. This will be a simple matter, as few herbs root as readily from cuttings. I often find small roots forming where thyme stems lie on the soil. These stems are an obvious choice for starting new plants. Just clip them from the main plant, being sure to get the portion with roots attached, cut back to

PHOTO BY JOHN TULLOCK

French thyme ready to sell

about two inches in total length, and stick the rooted end in the soil. Water well, and do not allow the soil to become thoroughly dried out. They should be showing new growth within two weeks. The flowers of all thymes are edible and make a lovely garnish, appearing in summer when the plant's flavor is at it tastiest. You can start some varieties of thyme from seeds, but with rooted cuttings so easy to produce, why bother? Like other herbs, thyme seedlings will vary in their culinary qualities. Vegetative propagation will insure that the flavor of your plants remains consistent.

Ornamental and Medicinal Herbs

If you find herbal products and herb gardening popular in your area (and it's catching on almost everywhere), consider some of the following as potential crops. As a rule, you will sell more of these herbs as potted plants than as bunches of cut herbs, with the possible exception of lavender. The list that follows includes only a smattering of the dozens of possible herbal crops.

Chamomile

An easily grown member of the aster family, chamomile prefers light, sandy soils and full sun. Too much nitrogen fertilizer will result in an overabundance of the feathery foliage at the expense of flowers. The latter, with bright yellow centers surrounded by white petals, hold up in bouquets, but are grown largely for dried product to use in teas. Chamomile tea is said to calm the nerves and promote sleep. Various references warn that chamomile promotes the same allergic reactions as ragweed. Those with a known reaction to ragweed should avoid both the living plants and chamomile tea.

Fennel

A perennial member of the carrot family, fennel can be both an herb and a vegetable grown for the bulbous stem base. The leaves, stems, and seeds have a distinctive licorice flavor. In warm summer climates, fennel does better as a fall crop, as it prefers cool, but not cold, temperatures. Healthy plants will resprout from the roots if frost does not kill too deeply. Like its relatives, fennel attracts swallowtail butterflies, whose larvae obtain potent protective chemicals from feeding on the aromatic oils present in their host plants. Gardening references repeat the advice not to grow fennel in close proximity to other plants. I have found that shoppers either love fresh fennel or avoid it like the plague. Try a test plot before committing much room to its cultivation. Fennel has naturalized in parts of the country with a suitable climate, such as coastal California.

Scented Geraniums

Legions of cultivars derived from several species make these cousins of window-box geraniums popular with many gardeners. As a rule, scented geraniums prefer full sun, good drainage, and high fertility. Potted plants need regular feedings of a liquid fertilizer, such as fish emulsion, while plants grown in beds should have plenty of compost. They are not frost hardy, and so must be provided with winter protection if you plan to grow them year after year. From Zone 7 south, the roots will survive if given a cover of mulch after cutting the plants back in late fall. They are evergreen in Zones 9 and 10. Desirable cultivars are produced from cuttings only, as seed does not come true. Scented geraniums provide a wealth of fragrances. A partial list includes: apricot, chocolate, cinnamon, coconut, ginger, lemon, lime, nutmeg, peppermint, pineapple, and rose. With over fifty cultivars of rose-scented geraniums alone, the possibilities for introducing customers to new ones are obvious. One interesting form is the mosquito plant, created through genetic engineering. By incorporating a gene from citronella into a lemon-scented geranium cultivar, science has given us a plant that supposedly repels mosquitoes.

Lavender

Two species, English lavender and French lavender, provide us with numerous lavender cultivars. English lavender is hardy in Zones 5 to 10, but suffers in the South's muggy summers. Two popular cultivars are 'Hidcote' and 'Munstead.' French lavender is recognized

Lavender

by the toothed margins of its leaves. It is not nearly as fragrant as English lavender but produces its lovely flowers more abundantly in hot, humid climates.

If you plan to grow lavender as a crop, learn which cultivar does best in your region. This herb has become popular in recent years, and has spawned clubs of fans anxious to learn its history, cultivation, and uses. Each summer my local club sells a mind-boggling amount of cut flowering stems at the local farmers' market.

Expanding Your Herb Gardening Horizons

Apart from those just mentioned, there are hundreds of other herbs for teas, home remedies, and a host of other uses. Owing to the plants' adaptability and people's widespread interest in all things herbal, herbs can provide a major, if not the main, source of income for your microfarm.

Key points to success with herbs are:

- Don't try to grow herbs that are poorly adapted to your region. Otherwise, cut herbs will be of inferior quality, and potted plants will disappoint your customers.
- Tuck herb plants anywhere in the garden suited to their needs. In order to have a continuous supply during the season, you will

need at least a dozen plants of each variety. For small plants, such as French thyme, several dozen will be needed.

- If possible, choose herbs that do double duty. For example, many culinary herbs produce colorful edible flowers as well as savory leaves, giving you two products for the effort of growing one.
- Make sure to provide customers with plenty of advice on growing (if you sell plants) and using herbs. You can do this via signage, flyers, or a website. Information regarding unusual varieties or new cultivars will be especially appreciated.

Small Fruits, Big Flavors

Among the many pleasures of the table, small fruits rank highly with most people. Although plant breeders have produced berry varieties that will withstand even international shipment to arrive in passable condition, locally grown ones simply taste better. Customers will have less waste with your fruits than with those brought from afar. Make certain to emphasize these points when selling. Most small fruits are extremely fragile and should be eaten within a day or two of picking. They are, therefore, good choices to provide a boost to your microfarm income. Not all small fruit cultivars are suitable for all areas of the country; indeed, different cultivars have been developed to thrive under the specifics of regional climates. You therefore should consult your state's agriculture extension service for information on the best choices. All the small fruits come from perennial plants and will need at least a season of growth before they bear a crop. Planting a patch of fruit for market represents an investment and requires careful planning.

Strawberries

No fruit exemplifies the abundance of regionally adapted cultivars more than the strawberry. Dozens of cultivars exist, and these come in one of three varieties. June-bearing strawberries produce a single crop in early summer; everbearing (or day-neutral) strawberries produce bumper crops in June, another smaller crop in

September, and a few berries all season long. Alpine strawberries, the third type, are closer to the wild berries from which all the other cultivars have been derived. They are everbearing, much smaller than the other types, and taste less sweet but more intensely "strawberry-like." Alpine strawberries can be grown in containers, while the others do best in beds. Alpine strawberries are the least adaptable to hot, humid regions of the country, as the "alpine" designation suggests, but will grow and produce a crop in most regions of the country.

June-bearing cultivars have received the most attention from breeders, resulting in strains adapted to all parts of the country. Much work has also been done with everbearing types, but you'll find fewer choices. Regardless of which varieties you choose, plan to move the strawberry patch every five years. This rotation is about the only way to avoid a plethora of problems. Strawberry plants tend to become exhausted after several seasons, leaving them prey to disease and pests that reduce yields significantly. If late spring frosts are typical where you live, you will need to grow a mid- to late-season berry cultivar or else plan to protect the blooms from frost damage with a row cover.

Planting methods vary depending upon whether you are growing June-bearing or everbearing strawberries. Either type needs full sun, well-drained sandy soil of slightly acidic pH, and an inch or more of water per week during the growing season. When preparing the bed, amend the soil with a two-inch layer of compost. Side dress June-bearing types with compost after harvest. Feed the everbearing varieties after their second harvest. Do not overdo the fertilizer, however, or you will get lots of foliage and few flowers. Never plant strawberries where any member of the tomato family (eggplant, peppers, tomatoes, flowering tobacco) has recently grown, or you risk infection with a type of rot known as verticillium.

Strawberries do not come true from seed. Obtain certified disease-free plants from a reliable source. Planting methods depend upon the type and the amount of work you are willing to invest in the patch. Because everbearing cultivars produce few runners, they are typically grown in hills spaced about a foot apart. Pathways between the hills should be at least two feet wide to allow easy access without compacting the soil and damaging the shallow root system. Remove runners from the plants as they form.

June-bearing strawberries produce abundant runners and are typically grown in wide rows, allowing some runners to take root and produce new plants. For the greatest yield, mother plants (the initial transplants you purchase) are set about eighteen inches apart in rows with two-foot-wide pathways in between. A maximum of two runners per mother plant are allowed to root. Choose surviving runners so as to keep all plants spaced a minimum of four inches apart, and ruthlessly remove all others. After the berries are picked, renovate the bed by mowing old foliage, side dressing with compost, and removing stray runners. Properly maintained, the bed should remain productive for five years, although the first year will always be the best one. Proper culture typically produces yields of about one and a half pounds of berries per square foot of growing bed.

Bramble Fruits

Bramble fruits include blackberries, boysenberries, dewberries, loganberries, and raspberries. All need to be grown on a trellis, and all need a season of growth before producing a crop the second year. (A few varieties will produce a minor crop the first season.) These members of the rose family produce fruit on the new growth borne on one-year old canes. After fruiting, the canes die and should be removed, both to prevent the spread of diseases and to make the planting more tidy and manageable. Do not compost the pruned stems, as they may harbor disease organisms. Instead, burn them or place them in the trash. Like strawberries, bramble fruits are so popular that plant breeders have developed cultivars suitable for all parts of the country, as well as different maturation times to extend the season. Raspberry cultivars are the hardiest, and will grow in Zones 3 to 9. Blackberries, dewberries, and loganberries are the most heat tolerant, Zones 5 to 10; loganberries grow best in Zones 6, 7, and 8. Consult your area cooperative extension service for cultivars suitable for your location.

Regardless of cultivar, bramble fruits require full sun and a deep, well-drained soil of average fertility and high organic matter content. All should be side dressed with a two-inch layer of compost each spring. Build your trellis before you plant. This can be a simple fence, a double fence, or a T-bar arrangement about four to five feet tall. The double fence works well for many gardeners, because it allows you to easily separate the canes by age, tying the new canes to one side and the old canes (which will fruit this season) to the other. Obtain plants from a nursery and set them about four feet apart, farther for the more robust varieties. Planting depth should be slightly deeper than when the plants were growing in the pot. Immediately cut the canes back to six inches to stimulate new growth. Mulch to conserve moisture, and scrupulously remove any weeds as soon as you notice them. (Weeding becomes progressively riskier to your skin as the thorny canes develop, so it pays to attack weeds early.)

Brambles need plenty of water, an inch per week until the fruit forms. Do not irrigate when fruit is colored, as this will reduce quality. During the season, separate the canes and tie them to the trellis. That fall, remove inferior canes to maintain a spacing of at least six inches, and cut back to about a foot taller than the trellis. The following season, the older canes will flower, and the plant will produce new canes. If you use the double fence type of trellis, you can tie the new canes to the side opposite the fruiting canes. Remove old fruiting canes after harvest. In fall, once again thin the canes and head back the ones left to grow. Maintain this cycle of pruning in subsequent years.

It is important not to prune too early. If the plants have not entered dormancy, pruning may encourage new fall growth that will be killed by early frosts, sapping the plants' strength. Yields vary with the cultivar and can range from one to eight quarts per plant. Red raspberries yield about one and a half to two pints per plant, for example. At $4 to $6 dollars per half pint, the return on your investment is highest for these most perishable of fruit crops.

Shrub Fruits

The most popular shrub fruit is the blueberry, but this group also includes currants, gooseberries, and some less familiar varieties such as elderberries and serviceberries. Besides producing an annual crop of delicious fruit, these plants are handsome enough to be used as hedges or specimen plantings. Always research preferred varieties for your region. Currants, for example, need cool temperatures and seldom do well south of Zone 6. None of the shrub fruits will perform well in the Deep South. For all shrub fruits, pruning is the key to maintaining healthy stands. Some blueberries, for example, lose a significant amount of productivity after the fourth year. Therefore, references recommend pruning out all five-year old canes. Low-bush blueberry types, on the other hand, fruit best on canes produced directly from the roots, rather than from buds on aboveground wood. Pruning is therefore done to encourage the former at the expense of the latter.

All shrub fruits need well-drained soil, plenty of air circulation, and abundant moisture. Blueberries are unique among the commonly grown fruits in their requirement for strongly acid soil. If your soil lacks natural acidity, you may need to prepare special beds for blueberries, keeping them well supplied with acidic components like pine needles.

You won't get quick results from the shrub fruits. Most need at least two seasons, and some blueberries need four, before they produce fruit. Once established, however, a well-grown stand of these plants can provide income each season for many years. Yields of course depend upon many factors. For southern highbush blueberries, the best type for my region of the country, about three or four quarts per plant can be expected. At $4 a pint, this works out to $6 or more per square foot of growing space.

Vine Fruits

Grapes, the king of the vine fruits, have been consumed since ancient times. As a result, there are countless cultivars. Some yield good table grapes, some are best for winemaking, and others are used primarily for jelly production. In addition, grape cultivars are perhaps the most regionally adapted of all food plants, with local adaptations determining whether you get a crop at all. Grapes need two to three years from planting to harvest. They also require trellising and careful pruning. They are not, therefore, the ideal choice for a quick return on investment. A grape arbor can be an attractive addition to the landscape, but I would give preference first to more productive plants. In terms of dollars per square foot, bramble or shrub fruits, which require about the same labor input, are a better deal.

If you live in an area with at least 150 days per year of frost-free weather, you might capture some of the novelty market by growing kiwifruit. The kiwi offers its own challenges to the intrepid gardener, however. Among these challenges is the need for both male and female plants. Only the females, of course, bear fruit, but the male will take up just as much space, thus reducing the yield per square foot. Two to three years are required for a planting to bear a crop. Like grapes, kiwifruit is unlikely to contribute significantly to the income of your microfarm.

Tree Fruits

If you are willing to endure the long wait for the crop, a small orchard can be a money factory. That said, be prepared to learn a lot before you take the plunge. For example, the climate in your area will determine which fruit tree species can be grown there. Don't expect lemon trees to grow in Ohio or apples in Florida. Beyond these basics, however, are a number of other factors that you must take into account. Foremost among these are "heating hours" and "chilling hours." These terms refer, respectively, to the number of hours per year when the temperature is above 65 degrees Fahrenheit or below 45 degrees Fahrenheit. If a fruit tree does not receive its particular requirement of chilling hours, it will fail to break dormancy in spring, and subsequently die. If the heating hours are insufficient, the plant fails to thrive, fruit fails to develop, and the tree usually dies after a few seasons. As if these complications were not enough, apples, pears, and cherries are usually not self-fertile, meaning they cannot pollinate themselves. Pollen instead must come from a different cultivar, and in many cases not just any old cultivar will do. Even the few self-fertile cultivars, such as the Montmorency cherry, produce higher yields if pollinated by a different variety. Thus, you need a minimum of two trees to produce fruit

Pruning fruit trees, a skill better developed with the help of a teacher rather than a book, is necessary if you expect production. This adds to your workload and is an annual chore.

Home-grown tree fruit will find customers at the farmers' market almost anywhere except in regions where fruit production is a major agricultural activity. However, unless you carefully research the project and commit to the substantial care these plants need, you will be better off starting other perennial crops on your property.

Edible Flowers

Whether used as a unique garnish or the featured component of a dish, edible flowers are worth growing and selling. I would not recommend them as a staple of your microfarm, but as a secondary crop they offer several advantages, among the most important of which is high value. A half-pint of edible blossoms is worth as much as the same amount of raspberries. But whereas raspberries produce a crop only during a narrow window in summertime, edible flowers can be harvested throughout the growing season in any climate, and year-round in the milder parts of the country. Many also make good cut flowers, allowing you to create small edible bouquets that can do double duty as both ingredients and table decorations.

The flowers of basil, chives, dill, geraniums, lavender, Mexican tarragon, rosemary, sage, and thyme are edible, too, and taste like the plant from which they came. Try offering them to restaurant chefs and at the farmers' market. Make certain before you try to sell them that you evaluate the taste, which can in some cultivars be overpowering. Choose your edible flowers carefully. Some common garden flowers contain harmful alkaloids and should never be eaten; a few are dangerously toxic.

Pick edible blooms early in the day and just before they open. Choose only perfect specimens and handle with great care. I place them in a single layer in a shallow plastic food container with slightly dampened paper towels lining the bottom. They will keep two or three days if refrigerated.

Arugula

The window for arugula as a salad green is narrow. Picked too early, the flavor is unremarkable. If you wait too long, however, the plants bloom, and the flavor become too strong. The difference can be only a few days. If you have a patch of arugula past its prime, pick only the flowers and add them to your product mix.

Bee Balm

Bees are not the only creatures that love the flowers of this perennial mint. Bee balm is native to the eastern United States and is also known as "Oswego tea." The flowers are bright red in the wild form and available in pinks, purples, and white in various cultivars. They add a citrusy note to salads and make beautiful garnishes. Pick the entire flower head, cutting it with about a foot of stem. To use, pluck the individual trumpet-like flowers. If you are thinking of growing one of the cultivars, be sure to evaluate the blooms for taste. This plant grows best in partial shade and moist soil. As with other mints, runners can be overly prolific and will fill a confined space. Every two years, dig, divide, and replant smaller clumps to keep it in bounds and productive. Insufficient moisture stresses the plants, typically bringing on a case of powdery mildew, although some cultivars are mildew-resistant.

Borage

The true-blue (sometimes pink) flowers of this annual herb have a cucumber-like flavor. Borage is a member of the tomato family. It grows two to three feet tall, and as wide. Start indoors in peat pots, or direct seed after all danger of frost has passed. Grow in full sun in rich, well-drained soil of average fertility. Borage plants also do a great job of attracting pollinators to the garden.

Calendula

Also known as "pot marigold," calendula is a cool-season daisy that grows readily from seed. In the South, it prefers a little afternoon shade (don't we all), but otherwise should have full sun. The flower petals can be added to salads, where their colors—various shades of cream, orange, mango, and yellow—provide an attractive contrast to the greens and reds of lettuces. Calendula petals can also be used in cooked dishes, where they impart the color (but unfortunately not the flavor) of saffron. The pollen-bearing flower centers should not be consumed by people allergic to ragweed.

Cucurbits

Squash and cucumber flowers are eminently edible. Squash blossoms were mentioned as a secondary crop in Chapter 8. While the female blooms with attached immature fruits are the most sought after, male flowers are tasty, too. Since they are also largely superfluous, you can pick them freely without worrying about reducing your yield of the fruit. Just make sure to leave a few on the plant to insure pollination.

Day Lily

Thousands of day lily cultivars exist, but not all of them taste good, so you must sample. Beware: too many can have a laxative effect. The wild type, *H. fulva*, is naturalized along roadsides and in meadows throughout the eastern United States. Dried "tiger lily buds" sold in Asian markets are, in fact, produced from day lilies. Picked the day before they open, the buds taste faintly like green beans and can be used in stir-fried dishes. Petals from fully opened flowers can be chopped and added to salads.

Caution: many "true" lilies contain toxic alkaloids and should never be eaten. Do not confuse them with day lilies.

Dianthus

Pinks, as these members of the carnation family are frequently called, will provide abundant blooms all season, mostly in white, red, pink, and combinations. Both annual and perennial varieties of dianthus are widely grown, the most familiar being sweet William. Seeds planted in fall will produce blooming plants the following spring. The cottage pink is a perennial suited to Zones 3 through 9. You can purchase plants or start seeds indoors for transplantation in spring after the frost date. Increase your best plants by rooting stem cuttings in summer. The spicy, clove-like fragrance is repeated in the taste of the flowers.

PHOTO BY JOHN TULLOCK

Hibiscus 'Disco Belle'

Hibiscus

Creative cooks use the large flowers of hibiscus as containers for fruit or vegetable salads. The blooms have a lemony taste, and in dried form are made into a beverage in Central America and the Caribbean. Add fresh ones, chopped, in small amounts to salads.

Legumes

While the flowers of garden beans, snow peas, and English peas can be eaten, many other legumes are highly toxic. Pea shoots, the tips of the vines harvested with or without flowers, are a delicacy and can provide an additional crop if you don't take too many from any one plant. The shoots of both English and edible-podded peas can be used. When the weather warms and peas begin to falter, you can salvage a crop of shoots before pulling up the plants.

Marigold

Although all marigolds are edible, most taste pretty bad. Gem marigolds are the exception, with citrusy flavors to complement their bright yellow and orange coloration. Grow them like other marigold varieties, starting seeds indoors for transplant, after all danger of frost is past, to a location in full sun.

Nasturtium

This is one flower that many cooks recognize as edible. Both leaves and flowers have a taste similar to watercress, a close relative. Nasturtiums grow best in cool weather and in soils of low fertility, making them an ideal choice for a marginally productive spot in the sun. Soils that are too rich will produce mostly foliage and few blooms. You can, in fact, evaluate soil conditions by the size of nasturtium leaves. If they are about two inches in diameter, the nitrogen content of the soil is okay for them, but will not support many other plant varieties. If the leaves reach four inches across, you can grow herbs or flowers that are not considered "heavy feeders." Leaves larger than four inches indicate soil of sufficient fertility for vegetables and other hungry crops.

Start nasturtiums from seed. They resent transplanting. Either sow where you want the plants to grow or start in peat pots a month before the last spring frost is expected, then transplant pot and all. Seeds overwinter in mild winter areas to sprout new plants the following year, but the flowers and foliage are killed by the first hard frost. Immature seed pods, as well as the flowers, can be used to flavor vinegar. The pickled pods are sometimes recommended as a substitute for capers.

Passionflower

The unmistakable blossoms of passionflowers make exotic table decorations, and petals can be added to salads or used as a garnish. Numerous tropical varieties exist, but the native *P. incarnata* strays into the temperate zone. It is an extremely vigorous perennial vine, worth having in the garden if there's room and a suitable support for its twelve to twenty feet of expansiveness.

HOW TO MAKE FLAVORED VINEGAR

Flavored vinegar offers the ideal way to preserve the taste of summer long after the leaves have fallen from the trees. Buy rice vinegar in bulk from Asian grocery stores. Try to find a local source for bottles and caps, or purchase them online. If you go the latter route, you'll pay a bit more for shipping. Pints are the most popular size.

Sterilize bottles by placing them upright in a boiling water bath canner, available at hardware and specialty stores. Fill the canner and the bottles with hot, not boiling, water, covering one inch above the tops. Bring the water to a boil and boil ten minutes. If you live more than 1,000 feet above sea level, add another minute for each 1,000 feet (or portion thereof) of elevation. Meanwhile prepare a draining rack. Use a sturdy dish drainer and wipe it down thoroughly with a mixture of one quart of tap water and one tablespoon of household chlorine bleach. Use the old-fashioned kind, not color-safe bleach.

When the bottles are ready, carefully remove them with tongs and drain them upside down in the prepared rack set over a sink. Bottle caps or corks should be placed in a saucepan of simmering water (180°F) for ten minutes, and kept there until you are ready to use them.

All vinegar products should have the words "Refrigerate After Opening" on the label.

PAY DIRT NASTURTIUM VINEGAR

Collect small, perfect nasturtium blossoms early in the day. Remove the stems within ¼ inch of the base of the flower and drop the blossoms into prepared bottles, adding 7 blossoms for each pint. Fill the bottles to within ½ inch of the top with rice vinegar. Cap the bottles, apply labels, and store them in a cool place until you are ready to take them to market.

Rose

Without delving into the special needs of rose plants, suffice it to say that their petals are edible. Roses have been cultivated and eaten for centuries. As a rule, the most fragrant cultivars also taste best.

Violets

Johnny-jump-ups, violets, and pansies are typical annual or perennial bedding plants that do well in most sunny gardens. They taste like mildly flavored cabbage and come in a spectrum of colors. These flowers have been eaten for centuries, and candied violet blooms are often sold in specialty shops for decorating cakes and other confections. Cultivars of the bedding types vary in their palatability. Some pansy blooms have an unpleasantly slimy texture, for example. As a rule, the smaller violas taste better. In milder climates, a fall planting will yield blooms all winter. They also have greater heat tolerance than pansies and will persist long into summer. Perennial garden violets are derived from many species, with several North American natives among them.

Cautionary Notes

As mentioned in the discussions of chamomile and calendula, flowers from members of the aster family should not be consumed by people with a history of allergies or asthma, as the pollen may provoke a severe reaction.

Furthermore, many common garden flowers are poisonous. Among the most dangerous are: azalea, crocus, daffodil, foxglove, jack-in-the-pulpit, lily of the valley, monkshood, narcissus, oleander, rhododendron, sweet pea, and wisteria. This is by no means an exhaustive list. Remember that just because one part of a plant can be eaten, this does not mean all parts can be. For example, tasty honeysuckle flowers mature into poisonous berries.

Always thoroughly research any plant before consuming it or offering it to your customers as edible.

chapter ten

Bank on Bouquets

For some of us, flowers on the table are as important a component of a great dinner as the vegetables are. Flowers also figure significantly in life's great transitions, marriages and funerals, and in celebrations of all kinds. Small wonder cut flowers always attract a crowd at the farmers' market.

Not all flowers stand up well in a vase. Some need special handling to increase their longevity. If you are a gardener, you may already grow many plants that bear good cut flowers. If you want to grow for market, experiment with new ones whenever you have the opportunity.

Making Sales Blossom

Inquire in your local florist shop about a possible market for cut flowers. Other possible outlets, besides direct selling at the farmers' market or from a street cart, include restaurants and caterers, wedding and event planners, craft shops, grocers, and online. Cut flower buyers will be looking for quality, diversity, and longevity in the vase.

Quality

Few products in your microfarm will test your skill as thoroughly as cut flowers. Customers want every bloom to be perfect. Top-quality flowers come from well-grown plants of suitable cultivars. Harvest them at the proper time in the plant's life cycle, and treat them with the utmost care from the time they leave the garden until you hand them over to your customer.

Diversity and Longevity

Professionals who frequently use cut flowers, such as caterers, are always looking for ways to distinguish themselves from their competitors. Using cut flowers that not everyone has seen before is one way they can accomplish this. If you can provide exotic or unusual blooms, you may be able to leverage the customer's interest in them into additional sales of the more mundane varieties. At the farmers' market, nothing attracts attention like a huge mixed bouquet, all the more so if the flowers are unfamiliar to the customers. Don't avoid flowers you know are standards, but always try to include something different in your offerings.

Customers want cut flowers to last as long as possible once they take them home. Assuring your cut flowers remain beautiful requires harvesting them at the correct time and treating them properly after cutting.

Harvesting and Conditioning

Choose flowers for cutting that have just opened or will open the following day. Once the pollen becomes loose enough to fall from the flower, it's too late to cut. Many references suggest cutting early in the day, but I have found flowers last longer when cut in late afternoon when the temperature has begun to fall. The plant spends the daylight hours making sugar via photosynthesis and uses the sugar during darkness. The leaves should have their highest sugar content, therefore, at sundown. Cutting at that time gives the flowers the benefit of the stored sugar. As a rule, the worst time to harvest is mid-morning to mid-afternoon, when the heat of the sun is at its most punishing.

Proper post-harvest conditioning is crucial to the quality of cut flowers. Take a bucket of water with you into the garden and immerse each stem as soon as it is cut. Protect the flowers from sun, and take them indoors for conditioning as soon as possible. Conditioning can be as simple as recutting the stems and transferring the flowers to a container of lukewarm water to which a floral preservative has been added. Some species, however, require special handling as discussed below.

Cut Stems under Water

Stems should be held under water when you recut them. This prevents the entry of air bubbles that would block the water-conducting xylem vessels within the stem. Remove the bottom two inches or so, making the cut at an angle to expose as much of the xylem as possible. Also, if you make a straight cut, the stem may sit snugly against the bottom of the container, inhibiting its ability to take up water. Use a sharp knife or pair of garden pruners to recut the stems. Scissors will crush the xylem. A clean cut will keep the xylem open, rather than collapsing it and interfering with water uptake. If the stem has nodes, as in carnations, make your cut between nodes.

Immediately transfer the stem to the conditioning container, which should be deep enough for the stems to be covered by about six inches of water. Remove all foliage that will be below water level during conditioning. Submerging leaves will result in rapid multiplication of bacteria, shortening the life of your bouquets. If the leaves are gray in color as in dusty miller, or fuzzy as in lamb's ears, be careful not to wet them, as this will produce discoloration. Instead, remove the lower third of the leaves and immerse the stems up to the remaining foliage.

Use Floral Preservative

The water used for conditioning should be about 110 degrees Fahrenheit. Add the appropriate amount of a floral preservative and mix well before placing the flowers in the water. The preservative provides sugar and prevents the growth of bacteria. Feeding sugar to the flower helps to maintain it in good condition. Bacterial growth will drastically reduce vase life, and gives the water an unpleasant odor. You can purchase premixed dry preservative at a florist supply house, but a homemade recipe work just fine and costs only pennies. To one gallon of water, add one tablespoon of sugar, a teaspoon of white vinegar, and one-fourth teaspoon of laundry bleach (the old-fashioned type, not the color-safe kind). The sugar feeds the blooms, the bleach is a disinfectant, and the vinegar provides acidity. Acid makes the preservative more effective by enhancing the ability of the plant to absorb water. Leave the stems in the conditioning water at least two hours, and preferably overnight.

Special Cases

Certain kinds of flowers need special handling. If the stems are woody, as with evergreen boughs or roses, scrape off the bottom half-inch of bark to expose the xylem. Then split the stem lengthwise once or twice with your knife. Do not crush the stem, as is sometimes suggested, because this is counterproductive. Remove all the foliage from woody plant stems.

Some plants produce a milky sap, designed by nature to seal off a wound. The sap will plug the xylem and prevent uptake of water. To prevent this, as soon as the stem is recut, hold it in a flame long enough to blacken, but not ignite, the stem tip. You can purchase a small propane torch for this task at any hardware store. A one-pound propane cylinder will flame hundreds of flower stems. The sap problem can also be foiled by holding the stem in boiling water for half a minute or so, but this method is impractical if you have many stems to treat. Poppies and milkweeds are examples of flowers notorious for their sticky sap.

Hollow stems, such as are found in delphiniums, hollyhocks, lupines, zinnias, and Queen Anne's lace, need more effort to keep them looking perfect for the maximum time. With a pin, pierce the stem just below the flower head (or the uppermost flower if a multiple bloom stem, like hollyhock). Then turn the stem upside down, fill with water, and plug the end with a small wad of cotton. You can also use a piece of florist foam as a plug. Return the filled stems to the conditioning container.

Bulbs, such as tulips and daffodils, should have the flowers pulled, not cut. Grasp the stem near the bottom and tug sharply. When you take them inside, recut the stem above the white portion that will be present at the bottom. Tulips will continue to grow after they are cut and will bend toward the light. To prevent this, wrap them in newspaper, secured loosely with a rubber band, before placing in the conditioning container. Make sure the newspaper is not in the water, as it will behave as a wick.

Daffodils produce a poisonous sap that will kill other flowers in the same vase. They therefore must be conditioned in a separate container. If you sell daffodils, you might want to remind customers of this problem. To create a mixed arrangement featuring daffodils, support the stems in florist foam, rather than simply placing them in water. The foam prevents the sap from leaking out and affecting other flowers in the same vase.

For flowers with soft stems, such as anemones and Lenten roses, remove all foliage and immerse the stems in the conditioning solution all the way up to the base of the flower head. Some flowers, such as hydrangeas should be completely immersed in water.

If you find that delicate blooms wilt during conditioning, try enclosing the exposed part of the plants in a plastic garbage bag to create a "mini-greenhouse." The humidity trapped within the bag will help prevent wilting. Tape the bag to the side of the bucket to keep it in place and to seal in humidity. Enclosing the blooms in this fashion also helps protect them during transport to the market.

Lilies produce large quantities of sticky pollen that rubs off and stains whatever it touches. If you've ever sniffed the delicious fragrance of an oriental lily and come away with an orange spot on the tip of your nose, you know what I'm talking about. When you recut a lily stem, be sure also to snip off the whole anther to avoid this problem.

Good Looks Sell Flowers

If you grow good quality flowers and find a market where the competition is not too stiff, you should have little trouble selling bouquets. To maximize sales, maintain your stand to keep it looking as professional as possible. Cleanliness is important, not only for appearance's sake but also to keep your flowers in their best condition. Make sure to clean your buckets thoroughly with soap and water each market day. White or green buckets will look best. You can often obtain white plastic five-gallon buckets at food service outlets free of charge. If you don't mind making the extra investment, florist supply houses carry containers in various sizes.

Packaging for Customers

Customers will want to get home with their bouquets without damaging them. You can purchase the same plastic sleeves that you see at the flower department of the supermarket, but newspaper works just as well. It also has the advantage of letting your customers know you care about the environment enough to re-use what would otherwise be a wasted material. A thornier problem is what to do when the customer wants a container of water to protect the blooms for a long journey. A plastic two-liter soft drink bottle with the top removed at the shoulder will serve the purpose. You probably have other suitable containers around the house. Always take along a couple, just in case. If the market does not have a supply of water available, you will need to bring some along. Plastic milk jugs work well, or purchase a five-gallon jerry can at a camping equipment supplier. Make sure you add floral preservative to the water.

Some flower sellers create mixed bouquets, while others keep different flowers separated and let customers decide. The grower I patronize most frequently does both. The choice is up to you, but make sure you offer a range of sizes and prices if you offer mixed bouquets. Otherwise, you may find that all the customers want a small nosegay on the day you show up with only $20 extravaganzas. In any case, always clearly post prices, and do not mix items of different prices in the same bucket. If you find that signage repeatedly gets damaged by water, use an indelible marker to write prices in large numerals on the buckets themselves.

Always explain to customers how to maintain the flowers in good condition at home. Daily changing the water in the vase is the simplest way to keep the flowers looking good. Give out the recipe for preservative. Above all, be friendly, courteous, and outgoing. Don't hesitate to give away freebies now and then. People will remember your kindness, and the cost is negligible.

Using natural and organic methods to produce flowers is just as important as it is for vegetable production. Be sure to tout your growing methods at the market. Put up signs, create a flyer about your flower farm, or just talk to customers about your approach.

Decide What to Grow

The list of potential cut flowers is not limited to the standard species, such as carnations and roses, that appear in any florist's window.

Everything from grasses to artichokes has been offered at one of my local markets. I suggest experimenting with anything and everything in your garden. Cut a few blooms and see how they hold up after overnight conditioning. The following lists should be taken merely as a starting point. I include some plants grown primarily for foliage rather than flowers. For varieties that are unfamiliar to you, simply type the name into a search engine to locate a wealth of growing information. Where particular cultivars are recommended, they are listed after the common name. Some popular genera are represented by multiple species, and some individual plant species have large numbers of cultivars. I've marked these plentiful plants with an "S/C." The absence of this indication, however, should not be taken to mean that only one variety is available.

Annuals and Biennials for Cut Flowers
- Ageratum, floss flower—'Blue Horizon,' 'Cut Wonder,' 'Florist's White'
- Bachelor's buttons, cornflower, bluebottle
- Bells of Ireland
- Calendula, pot marigold
- Cape marigold, African daisy, star of the veldt
- Celosias: cockscomb (S/C); feather celosia; wheat celosia
- China aster
- Cleome, spider flower
- Coleus (S/C)
- Corn cockle—'Milas'
- Cosmos—'Candy Stripe,' 'Double Click,' 'Seashells,' 'Sonata,' 'Versailles'; chocolate cosmos; yellow cosmos
- Dusty miller
- False bishop's weed—'Green Mist'
- Flowering cabbage, flowering kale
- Flowering tobacco, jasmine tobacco
- Foxglove; strawberry foxglove
- Globe amaranth (S/C); gomphrena—'Strawberry Fields'
- Licorice plant
- Love in a mist

Love in a mist

- Love lies bleeding
- Marigold, African marigold, Aztec marigold, big marigold, crackerjack marigold (S/C)
- Mignonette
- Painted tongue
- Snapdragon—'Rocket,' 'Bright Butterflies,' 'Supreme Double,' 'Madame Butterfly'
- Strawflower, immortelle
- Stock, gillyflower, ten-week stock (S/C)
- Sunflower—'Claret,' 'Italian White,' 'Ring of Fire,' 'Teddy Bear'
- Sweet pea (S/C)
- Sweet William (S/C)
- Zinnia (S/C); Mexican zinnia—'Aztec Sunset,' 'Desert Sun'

Perennials for Cut Flowers

- Alliums: chives; Chinese chives; star of Persia; lily leek; society garlic; giant allium
- Asters: New England; Michaelmas daisy—'Monch,' 'Wonder of Staffa'
- Baby's breath
- Black-eyed Susan (S/C)
- Canterbury bells, cup-and-saucer
- Cardinal flower (S/C)

PHOTO BY JOHN TULLOCK

Cardinal flower

- Carnation (S/C)
- Chrysanthemum (S/C)
- Coneflower
- Coral bells
- Coreopsis, tickseed
- Dahlia (S/C)
- Delphinium (S/C)

- Geranium (S/C)
- Gladiolus (S/C)
- Globe thistle
- Goldenrod (S/C)
- Hollyhock (S/C)
- Hydrangea—'Annabelle'; French hydrangea (S/C)
- Iris (S/C)

PHOTO BY JOHN TULLOCK

Japanese roof iris

- Lavender, French; English lavender—'Hidcote,' 'Munstead'
- Liatris
- Lilies (S/C)
- Lisianthus (S/C)
- Lupine (S/C)
- Peony (S/C)
- Phlox, garden (S/C)
- Pincushion flower

- Poppy, peony-flowered (S/C); Iceland poppy, arctic poppy; Shirley poppy, corn poppy, Flanders poppy; Oriental poppy (S/C)
- Red hot poker, torch lily (S/C)
- Snow on the mountain
- Speedwell
- Tuberose
- Tall verbena
- Yarrow, fernleaf—'Cloth of Gold'; milfoil (S/C); wooly—'Aurea,'; sneezeweed—'The Pearl'

chapter eleven

Nurse Your Finances

Some types of nursery stock make great crops for a small farming operation. Nursery products fall neatly into five categories:

- Annuals, including flower, herb, and vegetable plants
- Herbaceous perennials, including flowers, ferns, and some herbs
- Woody perennials, including vines, shrubs, and trees
- Floral products, such as poinsettias, that are sold in bloom
- Tropical plants, including houseplants and orchids

Time = Money

"Time is money" is an adage that is never more correct than when applied to the nursery business. The grower gets paid not for expertise but for the time required to take a crop from a seed, plug, cutting, or division to salable size. This can range from a few weeks in the case of annual flower and vegetable plants to several years for woody plants and slow-growers such as orchids.

Each of the crop's "life stages" offers a different level of risk and reward that the entrepreneur must take into account. For example, starting plants from seed is the cheapest way to obtain most species, but will also result in the highest percentage of losses. Some seeds may fail to germinate, seedlings may die young, and so forth.

You must also schedule your production appropriately. Avid gardeners will purchase blooming plants at almost any time of the season, but the majority of your sales will likely come in early to mid-spring. In some regions, there is a miniboom in sales in late summer to gardeners hoping for a beautiful fall display.

What's an Annual?

An annual is any plant that completes its life cycle in a single growing season. For the would-be nursery grower, product possibilities among the annuals include flower, herb, and vegetable plants. All are started from seed. Seedlings are usually grown under cover, in order to get a jump on the spring season. Packaged to facilitate transplanting by the retail customer, annuals make up a significant proportion of spring sales at garden centers, with the great majority attributed to flower plant sales.

Grow What Sells

"Color," as annual flowers are known in the nursery business, can be a reliable source of income. My favorite garden center sells tens of thousands of annual bedding plants each season, and most of them are the same varieties from year to year. I once asked the proprietor why they didn't try new and different cultivars, instead of producing thousands of the standard ones. He explained how foolish it would be to commit valuable greenhouse space to thousands of unproven sellers. They do experiment, he said, but usually with just a few plants purchased from other growers. This gives them a chance to see how customers will react to the new offerings.

My friend's explanation contains a message for the small grower Grow what sells. You'll be facing stiff competition from industrial-scale growers who can turn out plants by the millions, but if you carefully choose a market niche and grow quality plants, you can sell them.

Herbs

Annual herb plants can be a small but reliable income source. Parsley and basil typically dominate the sales. If you are growing basil or parsley plants for your own garden, you might as well grow extras to offer at the market. Select only the handsomest specimens. If the basil is leggy, it won't be as attractive to customers as a well-pinched, bushy plant would be. Stress can hasten the tendency of parsley to bolt, or go to seed, resulting in an unpleasant flavor. Thin early, so only one plant remains in the pot, and get it to market before roots appear in the drain holes. This will ensure that the plant does not quickly go to seed when the customer transplants it.

Vegetables

Vegetable starts are another good bet. The vegetables most commonly grown from transplants include broccoli, Brussels sprouts, cabbage, cauliflower, eggplant, peppers, and tomatoes. Beans, corn, cucumbers, okra, melons, and squashes can be grown from transplants if started in biodegradable pots that can be buried without disturbing the roots. Beans, corn, and okra are almost never offered this way, because you need at least a few dozen plants to obtain a worthwhile harvest. Nevertheless, some gardeners like using transplants to lengthen the growing season, even if only by a couple of weeks. Therefore, you could try starting okra, corn, or beans in cell trays and offering them by the flat.

Timing of vegetable starts is important. You cannot hold them in a flat for an extended time or they won't produce well. It is also important to have plants available at the proper time of year. Spring is the biggest sales season, of course, but more and more people are learning how to produce late season crops. I have often been disappointed to encounter a shortage of tomato and pepper plants after July 4 when I visit large garden centers, but I can find these plants at the farmers' market. The vendors there get my business because, being gardeners themselves, they understand what gardeners want. Strong, healthy broccoli and cauliflower plants for fall growing can also be hard to find when they are most needed, unless I shop at the farmers' market. It makes sense to grow extra plants and offer them to small local garden centers and at the farmers' market if you are already growing vegetable plants for your own use. Offer heirloom varieties overlooked by the mass producers, and time production to meet gardeners' needs.

Annuals in Containers

Another possibility for sales of annuals is to offer preplanted container gardens. For example, a single pot with basil, parsley, rosemary and oregano becomes an Italian herb garden in miniature. Marketing it this way makes it more attractive than calling it a "kitchen" herb garden. If you bring a little creativity to the project you can offer a whole array of themed miniature gardens.

Herb and Vegetable Themes

An Italian herb garden might look inviting in a classic urn, while an earthenware bowl could be home to a chili pepper "tree" surrounded by a "lawn" of thyme. Plant a big white pot with a single 'Patio' tomato surrounded with 'Spicy Globe' basil. Tuck in some oregano, and you have a Mediterranean-themed container. Once you get started, you'll be surprised how many designs you can come up with. Set yourself apart from the herd by using containers other than standard nursery pots. Look for containers at florist's supply houses, hobby shops, and outlet stores. Check out flea markets and yard sales for additional finds. To create a plant container, you can put drainage holes in almost anything that is both water resistant and amenable to drilling. Always wear eye protection and exercise extreme caution when working with power tools and breakable materials, such as ceramic flower pots.

Put your stamp of individuality on standard terra cotta and/or plastic pots by dressing them up with paint, applied decorations, or other artistic techniques. Check craft shops, craft fairs, and books to find ideas for personalizing containers.

Flower Gardens to Go

Extending the idea of preplanted container gardens from herbs and vegetables into the world of flowers opens up nearly limitless possibilities. When designing any container flower garden, keep some basic principles in mind:

- Plant only a few varieties per container.
- Use three basic plant types: spill, fill, and thrill.
- Pay attention to color harmonies.
- Have a theme in mind for each design.

You can create sensational containers with rather ordinary plants. In fact, plants for mixed containers should be hardy and reliable varieties. This is not the place for experimentation with untested crops, since a failure will leave a hole in the arrangement and a disappointed customer. Creating a few well-designed containers is a good way to use up a few extra plants when you've satisfied your own needs. And you can always purchase plants, if you find your design skills in demand.

Limiting Your Design

Diversity in a container planting suggests lushness, but only up to a point. For more than three plant varieties, you need a really large container. Even the basic trio should be given a ten- to twelve-inch diameter pot or larger. Otherwise, your arrangement will likely appear too "busy."

Spill, Fill, and Thrill

A good rule of thumb for container planting is to include a plant that will spill over the edge, softening the look of the container. Also include a plant with a spreading habit that will fill in the space among the other plants. And always supply a "thrill" by employing a focal point plant with dramatic height, bold foliage, a display of color, or a combination of these features.

Color Harmonies

You don't need an artist's color sense to design an attractive container planting, but it helps. Artists use the color wheel to balance each color with its opposite on the wheel. Thus, blue and yellow create harmony, for example. As with all such rules, of course, you need not adhere rigidly. Go ahead and combine salmon orange with coral pink if you think that will result in a salable container design.

Hanging Baskets

Preplanted hanging baskets offer another flower container possibility, especially if you have a greenhouse or large cold frame in which to produce them. Filling a ten-inch basket with a trailing flower and growing it to a state of abundant bloom in time for early spring sales is the way to go. Depending upon your climate, many possible plant choices work well in hanging baskets. Because a well-grown hanging basket can be difficult to transport without damage, you may find plenty of garden centers willing to take all you can supply, as long as you can deliver them in good condition. A grower of my acquaintance uses luggage bars in his van for this purpose.

Themes

Choose a theme for each container garden you create. For example, a container of red, white, and blue blooms might also have small flags to emphasize the patriotic theme. As with any other art form, the cleverer you are at this, the more likely you will achieve brisk sales. You will know you've succeeded when people approach you at the farmers' market about doing custom container gardens just for them. You may be surprised how much demand for this service exists if you live near even a medium-sized city. Take care to research the going rates in your area, so you don't undersell your time.

It is not necessary to grow everything you use. Approach your favorite garden center on a slow day and ask about trade discounts on plants you want to resell in container gardens. Independent garden centers will often extend a discount of around twenty percent to landscapers, growers, and others in the plant business. If you develop this kind of partnership with a center, be sure to reciprocate whenever you have the opportunity. For instance, you could recommend them to your customers as a reliable retailer. You may find yourself doing custom container planting for the garden center!

Herbaceous Perennials

If you are going to be able to earn some money selling nursery stock on a small scale, chances are the herbaceous perennials will constitute a large portion, if not the majority, of your business. Producing annuals requires more work than growing perennials and carries more risk, since annuals are highly perishable. At the end of the selling season, unsold annuals have no place to go but the compost heap. Perennials can be potted up and sold for more next year.

Mostly sold in a "trade gallon" container that holds about three quarts of growing mix, perennial flowers pack the displays of every garden center every spring. For some species, in my experience, demand always exceeds the supply. As with the other business strategies described in this book, growing perennials successfully requires you to discover what the market wants and then supply it. To narrow down your potential crops from among the hundreds of possibilities, choose one or two good garden centers in your area and ask them what plants they want but are unable to obtain from their usual sources. Another approach is to familiarize yourself as fully as possible with a particular group of plants, then assess whether your chosen group is adequately represented in the local outlets. Don't forget to include all types of outlets, not just garden centers, in your survey. Many grocery and hardware stores carry nursery stock in the spring, for example. Big box retailers and national chain stores are less likely to work with you than independent, locally owned businesses, of course, due to the former's need for enormous quantities of product, standardized packaging, bar-coded labels, and so forth.

Sources of Perennials

Herbaceous perennials may be grown from seed, from small plants called "plugs" and "liners" that you obtain from someone else, or from cuttings and divisions you take from stock plants you already own.

Seeds

Growing from seed will give you the most plants at the lowest cost, and you may be able to save seed from stock plants already in your garden. Obtaining the highest possible germination and survival-to-transplant rates, however, requires that you understand the specific requirements of each species you attempt to grow. Some species need light in order to germinate, others will sprout only in darkness. Some seedlings seem to leap from the soil within days, others may take weeks or even months to appear. Many perennial plants from the world's temperate zones require a winter chill before initiating germination, and some recalcitrant seeds need *two* winters' worth of cold before a shoot will emerge. If you aim to produce your own seedlings, you will obviously need to research the requirements of your target plants before you finalize your plans.

Seedlings are notoriously more fragile than more mature specimens of the same species. They need protection from drying out, temperature extremes, pests, and pathogens. Various fungi can attack seedlings during the critical stages of early development, for example, producing a condition known as "damping off." These fungi are helped along by improper growing temperature, excessive humidity, and poor air circulation. If you start plants in a green-house or indoors, the odds of damping off are greatly increased. On the other hand, starting seeds "naturally" in an outdoor propagation bed may result in spotty germination, and makes keeping track of your inventory more difficult. Nevertheless many of my perennial plants produce seedlings without my intervention, and I don't bother trying to start them indoors. It is a simple matter to dig and pot them for the following year's sales. I produce approximately half my stock from self-sown seedlings.

Plugs and Liners

"Plugs" are small plants grown in cell trays. Typically, a standard ten-inch by twenty-inch flat holds thirty-six plugs, but you can purchase trays with anywhere from twelve to 144 plugs, depending upon the size of the plants and the time you anticipate they will spend in the tray prior to transplanting. I find plug trays the most convenient way to manage seedlings that must be grown under protection, and I generally start the seeds directly in the trays. Some growers prefer to save space by starting seeds in smaller germination trays or pots, and then "pricking out" the tiny seedlings for transfer to cells or individual pots for continued growth. Handling plants this small requires more manual dexterity than I can typically muster, but if the seeds you have are in limited supply or are of an unusually valuable variety, or if they require some special treatment not needed for the majority of your plants, then germination in a small community tray or pot is the way to go.

"Liners" are small plants grown in individual pots (as opposed to the conjoined cells of a tray), intended for transplantation either directly into the garden by the consumer or into larger pots before eventual sale by the nurseryman. Where the standard flat of cells is ten by twenty inches, liner trays are typically seventeen by seventeen. Plugs are sometimes moved up to liners, especially if the intent is to sell the liner directly to the gardener. Groundcovers, herbs, and diminutive species such as violets are regularly sold directly to the public as liners. I often start seeds and cuttings in liner pots to avoid the labor of transplanting from cells or flats, particularly if I plan to sell the liner itself, rather than move the plant to a larger pot.

PHOTO BY JOHN TULLOCK

Liners ready for sale

Starting with a trade gallon pot might seem like the most economical approach at first glance, but it's not. The larger pots will need more room, more water, and more fertilizer, right from the beginning, than the equivalent number of liners. Each lost plant, therefore, takes with it considerable resources. You can recycle the pots and growing mix, but your water, space, and labor will have been wasted.

Many successful growers avoid the risks associated with starting their own seeds or cuttings by purchasing plugs and liners from specialty producers. They then grow these plants on for eventual sale. This can result in a tenfold increase in the value of the plant. Best of all, the time required to achieve a return on the investment is typically a year or less, where most perennials need two or more years from seed to produce a bloom.

Cuttings

Growing plants from cuttings that you remove from stock plants provides another cheap source of salable inventory. Cuttings are pieces of the stock plant that are handled so as to encourage them to produce new roots and shoots, growing into carbon copies of the plant from which the cutting is taken. As with seeds, the procedures needed to induce cuttings to root and grow range from the foolproof to the arcane. Research here is important. Some plants steadfastly refuse to root from cuttings, no matter how you attempt to cajole them into doing so. Others will grow roots if left lying on damp concrete. The key often lies merely in knowing the best time to take cuttings. Modern science has provided some assistance in the form of natural plant growth regulators known as "auxins." Treating a fresh cutting with auxin can increase rooting success manyfold.

The two auxins most commonly used by commercial growers are indole-butyric acid, or IBA, and napthaleneacetic acid, or NAAA. Some plants respond better to one or the other or a combination of both. Species-specific information can be found in propagation manuals. You can purchase liquid or dry preparations containing various formulations of these auxins under several brand names. Follow the label directions for treating your cuttings with these products. Don't make the common mistake of assuming that if a little auxin is good, a lot should be better. Too much auxin can actually inhibit root

PHOTO BY JOHN TULLOCK

Cuttings in liner pots

development. (Some herbicides work because they flood plants with auxins, completely deranging the plant's natural physiology.) As a rule, however, the more resistant the cutting is to rooting, the higher the concentration of auxin necessary to overcome the resistance. Young, soft cuttings from herbaceous plants will need far less auxin than tough, late-season stems from evergreens. The green summer branches of woody shrubs fall somewhere in between.

Over the years horticulturists have learned the most efficient way to propagate popular garden plants, and the information on specific varieties is widely available.

Cuttings most often come from the plant's stems, but other possibilities exist. For plants with thick, succulent leaves, such as begonias, a leaf can often be made to sprout new plants. One frequently used method is to remove the edges of a leaf with scissors, then make a series of short slits with a razor blade across, and perpendicular to, the middle vein. The whole leaf is then placed flat on the surface of a pot of growing medium and held in place with pins. The pot is placed in a humid chamber—enclosing it in a plastic bag works well—and set where it will receive light, but *not* in direct sun, which will cook the cutting inside its mini-greenhouse. The light should be just bright enough to read a newspaper. Rooting can take as long as six weeks or more, but some varieties may produce roots much faster. Another approach is to use a hole punch to remove circles of tissue from the leaf along the midvein, treating the circles with auxin before placing them on the surface of a growing medium. Still another approach is to root a leaf with a piece of its stem still attached by placing the stem end directly in water.

If you don't like the idea of using a bottle of chemicals to help your cuttings root, try the natural approach with "willow water." Willows are notoriously easy to root. Even willow "stems" as large as four inches in diameter will root in moist ground. Willow switches gathered in spring will root in plain water within a couple of weeks, and the water will be rich in natural auxins. People long ago learned that other cuttings would root quickly in this water, and many of us use the method to this day.

Cuttings can also be taken directly from the roots of some species. A stock plant is dug, one or more roots is removed, and the plant is returned to the soil. The roots are cut into short segments that are placed in pots on or the surface of a flat of growing mix. Auxins may or may not be used. For some species, such as Virginia bluebells, even a tiny piece of root will regenerate. (Gardeners plagued with the invasion of a flowerbed by certain weeds know this all too well.)

Divisions

The most straightforward way of propagating herbaceous perennials is simple division. Lift the plant from the soil and separate it into several smaller plants with both roots and leaves attached. These divisions are then replanted in pots. Within a few weeks, if all goes well, you have multiple plants where once only one grew.

As usual, plants vary in their response to this treatment. Success depends not only upon the nature of the plant but also upon the timing of the operation and the care expended upon the new plants in their first weeks of life. Summer, as a rule, is a poor time to divide anything, because high temperatures and intense sunlight may damage or kill the divisions before they can become established. Exceptions are early summer bloomers like irises and day lilies. Divisions from these are usually made in summer, shortly after the blooms have faded. Some plants benefit from division in the fall, as they prepare to go dormant, or have already entered dormancy, to ride out the winter months. Other plants—for example, hardy ferns—do best when divided in early spring, when they are growing new roots. Fall division of ferns may result in losses, as the plants will just sit in the ground for several months without producing roots. Exposed to drying winter winds without a fully developed root system, they may not survive. Spring, just at the time new growth appears, is the best time to divide most herbaceous perennial plants. For fall blooming varieties, divisions taken in early spring will often be in bloom, and therefore salable, by the end of the same season. Spring and summer bloomers will generally skip the first year before blooming again the following season.

Because selling plants out of bloom can be difficult, even if they are otherwise superior specimens, keep these points in mind when planning the timing of your micronursery operation.

Marketing Perennials

"The bloom sells the plant" is an old adage in the nursery business. Especially in spring, gardeners want to return home from your market stand or local garden center with plants that are already in bloom or soon will be. Therefore take it as given that you should be prepared to offer budded or blooming plants.

Labeling

If you must sell plants out of bloom, consider purchasing pot labels featuring a color photo. Preprinted "pot stick" labels are available for hundreds of standard perennial cultivars. You can also buy stock labels from mail-order suppliers. You can purchase blank pot sticks supplied in break-apart sheets. These allow you to print your own labels using a computer. Large nurseries use expensive thermal printers, economical only for runs of thousands of labels, but you can make do with a printer from the office supply store. Many liquid inkjet printer inks will not stand up to nursery use, but innovations appear all the time, so check with various manufacturers to find printers offering the option of water- and UV-resistant ink. Laser printers may offer you the widest range of options, as laser toners usually hold up well outdoors. Nevertheless, if you go this route make sure to check with the manufacturer regarding the ultraviolet resistance of its toners. Because the world of computer hardware is constantly changing, it is impossible to give specific suggestions for a printer.

Another possibility for labels is to print your information on an adhesive label that you then apply to a standard nursery tag or pot stick. Here again, you'll need to make certain the ink or toner will stand up to outdoor use. Also, the label adhesive must be waterproof.

You can go a step further and order pot sticks or tags preprinted with your nursery name and contact info on one side, then apply the customized adhesive label to the other side. This costs more, of course, but is still cheaper than custom-printing labels for each variety.

One grower I know uses hand-lettered labels and provides plant photos and other information on a website. You could also compile a photo album to take along with you when you go to the farmers' market. When customers ask what the blooms look like, you can whip out your trusty album. You can also create signage that includes a photo and cultural information. Several vendors at my local markets make paper signs and then have them laminated in plastic at an office supply store. Signs such as these will last about one selling season before they need replacing.

Information Sells Plants

You may prefer to sell nursery stock only to garden centers, even though you must sell at a lower price than retail. One of the benefits of selling your plants wholesale is that the task of answering gardeners' questions falls to the garden center staff, while you get to go home and garden. Not so if you sell retail at the farmers' market. In the retail plant business, information will be one of your most important "commodities," and you probably won't get paid a cent for it. Perennials do not merely represent a greater investment per plant for the customer. Because perennials return season after season, gardeners want some assurance that the plant will adapt and thrive when they take it home. It is the expectation of long-term value that fuels the demand for information. Especially if you offer plants or varieties that are in any way unusual, expect to get a ton of questions before you make sales. Besides the usual sun-or-shade? wet-or-dry? queries about cultivation, you will also need to know the plant's height, bloom time, hardiness, and just about anything else you can compile regarding its cultivation. Customers will appreciate receiving a slip of paper with a summary of the basic information. Producing this kind of sales aid costs little and can be done with any computer and a copier.

Find a Specialty Niche

You may be able to carve out a niche for yourself in the local garden marketplace if you specialize in one or a few types of perennial plants. Among the more popular subcategories you might consider are plants native to your region, plants that attract butterflies, fragrant plants, or plants of a certain color. The famous White Flower Farm, for example, began by offering only plants with white flowers and has now grown into a major supplier of perennials in all colors.

Shade Plants

If you lack sun, you can specialize in plants that perform best in shade. Among the most popular of these are ferns and hostas. Hostas are generally easy to grow, multiply rapidly by division, and adapt to a range of conditions. The problem with them, from the grower's point of view, is that the market is often flooded. Common sense suggests that any plant so easy to grow will be widely represented in the marketplace. Seek out cultivars that are not commonly available in your area.

Ferns can be more precise in their requirements, but nevertheless may be a profitable choice for a crop. You can order liners of many varieties of ferns, transplant them to gallon containers, and sell them at a profit the following spring.

PHOTO BY JOHN TULLOCK

Japanese painted fern

Ferns from Spores

You can also, if you are adventurous, grow many ferns from spores. Unlike flowering plants, ferns have a unique life cycle that begins as a nearly microscopic spore. Underneath the fern leaf, you have undoubtedly observed the dark colored "fruitdots," or sporangia, that contain the spores. When the ripe spores are sown on an appropriate medium with adequate moisture, they germinate to produce a tiny, unimpressive structure called the prothallus. The prothallus, in turn, develops male and female structures analogous to the stamen and pistil of a flower. (In some species, the male and female structures are borne on separate prothalli.) Sperm cells produced by the male part of the prothallus swim to the stationary female structures to accomplish fertilization. This phenomenon explains why ferns are typically found in moist habitats. Even ferns that inhabit dry climates must have water to reproduce. These species often time their reproductive cycles to coincide with seasonal precipitation. Once the egg is fertilized, a new plant grows from the prothallus, which, its vital function complete, then dies. The new plant will be a perfect replica of the parent fern in miniature. When it reaches a size large enough for convenient handling, the plantlet can be potted up and will proceed to grow into a mature plant, usually within two to three years' time. Smaller specimens can be sold as liners, in three- or four-inch pots, while most mature ferns are sold in gallon containers or larger. If you have the skill and patience to grow ferns from spores, you can produce many hundreds of plants from a single frond at low cost. Exact specifications for growing many species of ferns from spores can be found in various references. Some of the better fern books are mentioned in the Appendix, along with some fern websites. If you decide to explore the wonderful world of ferns, you will discover that fern enthusiasts have been swapping spores for many years. This can be one of the best ways to acquire new varieties for your collection of stock plants.

Not all ferns reproduce easily from spores, and some spores must be very fresh in order to germinate. Many otherwise highly desirable hybrid ferns do not come true from spores or do not produce viable spores at all. These must be produced by division of mature plants, or, more commonly these days, via tissue culture. Tissue culture is the source of many fern liners offered in the trade. Theoretically, you can do this at home, but you will be better off buying liners from the tissue lab and growing them out, unless you are prepared for the sizable investment in equipment and materials, plus the time required to master the techniques.

Butterfly Plants

In recent years, concerns over the decline of local ecosystems have resulted in great enthusiasm for gardens designed to attract butterflies. Two types of plants are involved, those that provide nectar for the colorful adult butterflies we all love to watch, and those that provide food for the caterpillar. Adult butterflies are attracted to both types of plants, so butterfly gardeners cultivate plants like parsley and nettles for the caterpillars, in addition to nectar plants like salvias and phlox for the adults. You can capitalize on this trend in various ways. Nectar plants are often standard perennials and don't necessarily have to be native to the same area of the world as the butterflies feeding on them. I've seen local butterflies visiting the flowers of my tropical orchids that originate in rainforests thousands of miles from Tennessee. Nectar is nectar, apparently. Caterpillar host plants, on the other hand, may be extremely specific. The familiar monarch butterfly, for example, places its eggs only on certain

PHOTO BY JOHN TULLOCK

Gulf fritillary

members of the milkweed family, while the spicebush swallowtail caterpillar feeds on the spicebush shrub and the sassafras tree. The range of any butterfly is limited by the range of its caterpillar host plants. For example, the Gulf fritillary feeds on members of the passionflower family.

Most passionflowers are tropical, but *Passiflora incarnata* has extended its range into the temperate zone. Wherever the plant grows, the butterfly follows, having been spotted as far up the Atlantic coast as Delaware, dutifully searching out blooms of passionflower vines in the gardens of native plant enthusiasts. The adults favor such nectar plants as tall verbena and Drummond phlox. You can learn about the butterflies in your area from a good regional field guide, or from the numerous websites for butterfly devotees. Suggestions for both are included in the Appendix.

Native Plants

Native wildflowers offer you another option for specialization. The last two decades have seen a steady increase in demand for nursery-propagated natives. In years past, most native wildflowers were dug in the wild. This reprehensible practice continues, but is on the wane as more nurseries produce indigenous plants. Growing nursery-propagated wildflowers benefits the local environment by providing food for many types of wildlife. Wildflowers also participate in biological give-and-take with soil microbes, fungi, and invertebrates, encouraging the development of a healthy soil ecosystem. Once established, a garden of native plants needs less care than a conventional garden, because the plants are already adapted to the vagaries of the local climate. For example, growing natives in the desert Southwest can reduce the garden's demand for irrigation water. Wildflower gardening not only maintains the genetic diversity of the species being grown, but also supports populations of pollinators and predators.

Wildflowers are also great "ambassadors" for the whole ecosystem in which they live. When people have an opportunity to see, touch, and smell local wildflowers, they become more aware of their regional botanical heritage, and thus more likely to support the preservation of natural wildflower stands in parks and reserves. Botanical gardens now routinely feature displays of regional plants. Indeed, some public gardens are devoted solely to showcasing natives.

PHOTO BY JOHN TULLOCK

Virginia bluebells, a popular native flower

Like other herbaceous perennials, you can propagate native wildflowers by several means, including seed, cuttings, and division. If you know of a stand of native wildflowers on private property, you can with the owner's permission collect seed or cuttings for propagation purposes. I have also been known to collect seeds along rural highway rights-of-way. You will also be pleasantly surprised to discover, as you delve into the world of native plants, how many popular garden perennials are native to the United States. Bluebells, phlox, asters, sunflowers, salvias, and lobelias are but a few examples from east of the Mississippi.

Don't overlook native grasses. Besides adding their special beauty to the garden, they can be some of the most durable plants around. America's Great Plains once harbored millions of acres of native grasses, like big bluestem and switch grass. Today, with these natural stands largely replaced by corn and soybean fields, native grasses are a welcome addition to the wildflower garden.

If you decide to grow and sell native plants as part of your product mix, make certain to tout their many values in all your marketing efforts. Also, be prepared to answer plenty of questions from gardeners new to wildflower cultivation, particularly if you are introducing them to unfamiliar species. Pot tags and/or flyers with cultivation tips are essential. Display your plants in groups of garden companions. Plants that like damp shade can all be grouped together, for example, while plants that prefer a well-drained, sunny spot can compose another group. This is one of the best ways to encourage novice wildflower gardeners to develop enthusiasm for your products.

To get started with native plants, check out a good wildflower guide from your local library, and familiarize yourself with the plants of your region. Numerous online references to gardening with natives are also available. See Appendix.

Fragrant Flowers

A casual stroll along the benches in any garden center will reveal that a substantial proportion of the flowers offered are hybrids. This has been a great boon to horticulture, but too many modern flowers have lost their fragrance due to excessive hybridization. Petunias provide a good example. Old-fashioned petunias have a charming scent, while their hybrid counterparts might as well be made of silk. Fortunately, enough gardeners want to be able to stop and *really* smell the flowers,

PHOTO BY JOHN TULLOCK

Fragrant ladies tresses, a hardy orchid

and fragrance is making a well-deserved comeback. Investigate fragrance as a way of distinguishing yourself in the marketplace, and you may happily discover that you have a winning strategy. Both annual and perennial varieties can be included in your repertoire. Although you may have to do some hunting to locate seeds or stock plants, fragrant plants almost sell themselves. If you go to the farmers' market with a huge display of plants in bloom, customers may find their way to your stand with their noses alone.

Few other groups of plants offer so much opportunity to the suburban grower than the herbaceous perennials. Whether you specialize in one of the areas mentioned above, develop your own ideas, or simply grow top quality plants of the old standbys, your inventory will find a ready market almost anywhere.

Woody Perennials

Trees, shrubs, and vines are the backbone of any landscape. Producing them can be a lucrative business, provided you are patient. Most woody plants require five years or more to produce a salable plant from seed, and two to three years from a cutting. If your aim is quick cash, woody plants won't be your first choice. On the other hand, if you like the idea of literally watching your money grow, planting a crop of trees or shrubs in containers and waiting for them to get large enough to sell can be a rewarding experience. As with any other crop, however, you need to make certain that a ready market exists for the mature plants.

Seedlings

As mentioned previously, the size of the container controls the price you can charge for a woody plant. Seedling trees, for example, probably will not repay your time to grow them, because they can be bought for less than a dollar apiece, even in small quantities. There are exceptions, such as trees whose seeds do not germinate readily. For example, the fringetree requires two seasons to produce its first leaf. Year one is spent developing a root, and the shoot appears only during the second spring. After year two, the fringetree grows slowly for another couple of years before reaching a salable size. If you have the seeds and the patience, you can sell every fringetree you produce. To find out what might sell well in your area, try asking the proprietor of a good garden center what species are in short supply.

Cuttings

Cuttings produce salable plants faster, usually within two years after the cutting is taken. There is a downside, however. Stock plants can be severely harmed if too many cuttings are taken, or if they are taken too frequently. This obviously limits the productivity you can achieve, especially if you have only one plant to work with.

The key to getting woody cuttings to root lies in knowing when to select stock. The appropriate time ranges from late spring far into autumn. One of the best books on the subject is Michael Dirr's *Manual of Woody Landscape Plants.* Dirr provides precise protocols for propagating just about every tree, shrub, and woody vine species grown in temperate North America. As you read his explanations you will note that the best time for taking cuttings from a given species varies from year to year, depending upon the weather.

A few years back, all of my stock plants were seriously damaged by an unusually late freeze. Plants from which I could normally have taken cuttings in June did not develop sufficiently for the purpose until August. Thus, it behooves the micronursery grower to learn how to tell when cuttings should be taken by observing the plant. In most deciduous species, wood for cuttings should have just begun to harden. Cuttings that are too green may rot before they root, and cuttings past their prime may refuse to root at all. I have a Florida anise tree that does not develop new growth until late summer, for example. Its stems are not ready for cutting until September or October, long after most shrubs have become too mature to root.

Evergreen cuttings are typically taken in fall or early winter, when the stems have fully matured. Some evergreens never root from cuttings, though, so do your research. If your plants are large and healthy, and you don't require huge numbers of cuttings, you can hedge your bets by taking cuttings sporadically over a period of weeks.

The process of taking woody plant cuttings is similar to that for herbaceous plants. Applying an auxin before placing the cuttings in rooting medium is almost always necessary. While herbaceous cuttings can be potted up as soon as the roots are sufficiently developed, disturbing newly rooted woody cuttings can cause them to enter a premature dormancy from which they never emerge. Therefore, cuttings rooted this summer typically should not be transplanted until the following late winter or early spring, when the plants would normally be breaking dormancy.

Growing On

You can bypass the wait for seeds and cuttings to develop by purchasing small plants and growing them on in your micronursery. Especially if you want a diverse inventory for farmers' market sales, this may be your best option. A seedling you purchase for fifty cents will be worth $10 when it is large enough to occupy a three-gallon nursery can.

For an even quicker turnaround, check with your local garden centers and DIY stores late in the season for overgrown plants and leftovers from the spring rush. Often these plants are marked down significantly in price, and you may be able to negotiate an even larger discount for a quantity purchase. Many garden centers lack the time and staff to pot up hundreds of plants. At the end of the season, the leftovers are tossed into the dumpster. Salvaging these plants and potting them on can produce a 100 percent return on your investment the following spring. Always remember, it's the container, not the plant, that determines the price. An overgrown plant in a gallon can will sell for twice as much if it is merely moved up to a three gallon can. Please do not try this at home. It will cost you customers.

Floral Products

Potted plants sold in bloom and intended for use as indoor decorations compose the "floral product" nursery category. The ubiquitous Christmas poinsettia provides the most familiar example. Other seasonal staples include miniature roses for Valentine's Day, Easter lilies, Mother's Day azaleas, and the like. The vast majority of these plants are produced in factory-like settings at very low cost. Therefore, you will need to be either unusually creative or unusually lucky to make any money growing them on a "micro" scale.

But you need not grow poinsettias. Be creative. Follow the suggestions offered earlier in this chapter for mixed container gardens. Develop your own ideas for seasonal blooms. I found myself with an overabundance of bulbs of 'Orange Pixie' lilies one season recently. Instead of composting the extras, I potted them up. Adding a white florist sleeve and bow resulted in the perfect choice for fans of the locally beloved University of Tennessee sports teams, whose colors are orange and white.

Tropical Plants

Tropical plants are those that cannot survive the winter outdoors in the temperate zone. If you think you need a greenhouse to produce tropical plants, you should see my orchid-growing space in the garage. Like many other tropical plant lovers, I grow various orchids and other plants under fluorescent lights. I also grow on sunny windowsills.

If you are fortunate enough to own a greenhouse, you probably have already considered using it to produce plants for sale. Indeed, some of my gardening friends have successfully used the promise of plant sales to justify to their spouses the investment in the greenhouse. I make no guarantees regarding your domestic relations, but a greenhouse can pay for itself pretty quickly if properly managed.

The standard advice for commercial greenhouse production is to grow one or a few crops in quantity, rather than going for a diverse inventory. If you have a specific market in mind, or better yet an agreement with a garden center for next season, the "all eggs in one basket" approach can work. Its advantages include a uniform set of conditions for the entire house, including a predictable schedule of irrigation, fertilization, and other necessary chores. On the other hand, if you are growing for your own market stand, you probably cannot use 500 Boston ferns, and a greater diversity of inventory makes more sense. Be sure to research potential markets before you commit.

One big plus offered by tropical plants to the microfarmer is that they grow quickly, meaning that you can often go from cutting or liner to marketable size in only a few months. Orchids are the most notable exceptions to this rule, typically requiring a year or more to mature from a liner.

Tropical ferns grow rapidly and sell well

Tropical ferns grow much faster than orchids. Purchase liners and grow them out for sales the following year. Tropical ferns can also be started from spores, but this extends the time required to obtain a mature plant.

Ferns in hanging baskets find a ready market in my area. Many people decorate the porch with a fern basket or two in summer, and then toss the plants when frost arrives. Ergo, these customers will be back for more next spring.

Exotic tropical floral products—from heliconias to zingibers—may be just the ticket in your market.

Orchids

One floral product group that always attracts attention is the orchid family. Orchid growing can be a great source of extra income. It is important that you understand their special needs, but the techniques are easy to master. Observe the usual precautions about finding a market before you take the plunge. In general, orchids are slow growing, requiring anywhere from three to five years to produce a blooming plant from seed, but they also can command a substantial retail price. A blooming orchid in a six-inch pot can sell for as much as a tree in a five-gallon can.

With possibly 30,000 naturally occurring species and many tens of thousands of hybrids, narrowing down the possible crop selections among orchids is a daunting task. You must first decide whether you want to market plants to the general public or to orchid fanciers. If you have extensive experience with orchids, you will understand the factors, such as winning an award from the American Orchid Society, that determine the value of a particular plant. Thus, you may have good luck selling to other orchid enthusiasts. If you are just getting started, on the other hand, you will be better off targeting the general public with easily grown hybrids. Many orchids make excellent houseplants, and these are the varieties upon which you should focus. By far the most popular ones are *Phalaenopsis* hybrids. Also known as "moth orchids," *Phalaenopsis* produce long-lasting flowers in almost any color or combination

Phalaenopsis equestris, an easily grown tropical orchid

you might imagine except blue. They grow rapidly and adapt well to conditions found in the average home. You can order small plants from a supplier, bring them into bloom, and sell them for a profit within a year.

While a heated greenhouse is the ideal orchid-growing space, many of the most popular types can be produced under artificial lights. Besides *Phalaenopsis*, you could select from among the genera *Brassavola, Brassia, Cattleya, Dendrobium, Oncidium,* and *Paphiopedalum*, just to name a few. Hybrid genera, such as *Brassocattleya*, a cross between *Brassavola* and *Cattleya*, combine the floral qualities of their parents, and as a rule are more amenable to cultivation than are natural species. Most orchid floral stock consists of hybrid plants. Two inexpensive fluorescent light fixtures, each holding two forty-watt lamps, will illuminate six square feet of growing space. That is plenty of room for several hundred dollars' worth of stock.

You can obtain inventory for your orchid nursery in the same way as with other plants, and with the same risks and rewards. Orchid seeds, nearly microscopic in size and devoid of stored food for the developing embryo, must be started under laboratory conditions on sterile growth media. Growing orchids from seed, therefore, is best left to the experts. However, you can purchase small seedlings at low cost, grow them out, and realize a substantial profit after, typically, two to three years of growth. The smaller the plants at the time you purchase, the less they will cost you, but your losses between seedling and sale will be proportionately greater. Orchid seedlings are enormously more sensitive to desiccation, disease, and improper culture than are their mature counterparts.

chapter twelve

Go Beyond the Mainstream

Your suburban microfarm can take whatever form, and produce whatever products, you think make the most sense. Listed here are a few more ideas, including some off-the-wall ones.

Honey

Because bees pollinate a host of crops in addition to providing honey, keeping a few hives is a win-win for any farmer. Before you take the plunge, though, check with the appropriate local authorities to find out if beekeeping is permitted under the zoning regulations that apply to your property. Also find out what health department permits you may need in order to put up your honey in jars and sell it to the public. You will also need to make a considerable investment in hives, protective gear, the bees themselves, and so forth.

Bulk Herbs

Herbal products are used in prodigious quantities. If you have the proper growing conditions and enough space, you might want to consider devoting your efforts to a single, high-value crop. The possibilities are legion. If your soil is well drained and your climate mild, lavender is a crop possibility. It is widely used for making artisanal soap and other toiletries.

Honeyleaf bears insignificant flowers and leaves sweeter than sugar

If you live where rain is plentiful, summers are long, and the soil is rich, consider honeyleaf. This South American herb has been used as a sweetener for centuries. The plant is many times sweeter than sugar, but with zero calories. You will need to locate a processor interested in purchasing your honeyleaf crop, and, indeed, this is the only wise approach to growing any bulk herb product.

Eggs

As anyone who has sampled one will tell you, nothing tastes quite as good as a farm-fresh egg from a free-range chicken. The pale-yolked, lackluster examples found in the supermarket case simply cannot compare. To the farmer's advantage, people are willing to pay $3 for a dozen really good eggs. My neighborhood has a proscription against keeping chickens, and many locations prohibit the practice outside of areas zoned for agriculture. However, attitudes are changing. Living in Manhattan, for example, are thousands of chickens tended by devoted fans. Across the country, groups of chicken fanciers have successfully challenged local laws that restrict the keeping of poultry on a small scale. A vast body of information on the national network of urban poultry farmers, as well as suppliers of chicks and poultry supplies, is accessible online. See the resources in the Appendix for some links.

As is the case with beekeeping, raising chickens involves an investment, and selling eggs may require health permits, inspections, and similar trappings of bureaucracy. Check with your local health department, your state department of agriculture, or your cooperative extension service for information specific to your area. Neighbors will certainly complain if your poultry project results in noise or unpleasant odors. Odor problems can be avoided by proper management. Chicken manure must be composted before it can be used on crops. It is too "hot"—that is, too rich in nitrogen—to be used as a fertilizer when fresh. Combining chicken bedding with other compost ingredients should reduce odor production considerably. Noise should only be an issue if you have a rooster. Sexing a chicken is a job for well-trained experts until the bird is old enough to display secondary sex characteristics, usually between four and six weeks of age. After they have been around for a time sufficient to separate the ladies from the gentlemen, it may be difficult for you or your family to part with the little buggers. Nevertheless, part with them you must, as roosters will fight each other and in any case are needed for no purpose other than fertilization. If it seems likely in your case that family protests will arise if you carry out summary executions, pay a bit extra for birds that have already been sexed. Females are called "pullets" in poultry lingo. Baby chicks have been shipped from hatcheries via mail order for years, and many people obtain their birds that way. You can also check the classified ads for local sources of birds. These will be breeds well adapted to your region, but you may not have the choice of sexed chicks.

Foraged Products

You can supplement the income from your microfarm with foraged items. If you sell cut flowers, for example, you may have a market for cones, driftwood, gnarled branches, seed pods, and similar things that you can harvest from natural stands with the property owner's permission. Protect yourself by getting that permission in writing. Always respect the landowner and the land by taking only what you reasonably need.

Perhaps the most valuable foraged product is wild mushrooms. Even in some protected areas, mushroom hunting may be permissible. **However, no one should harvest mushrooms for human consumption without absolute certainty of their identity**. Deadly poisonous species can often look nearly identical to harmless ones. Identification of wild mushrooms requires training—**you cannot rely on a book to learn this skill**. Joining a mycological society is the best way to get the knowledge you need, or you can take classes for a fee.

Cultivated Mushrooms

Cultivating mushrooms is another matter altogether from foraging. You can order mushroom spores, or "spawn," from various suppliers. Then you use the spawn to start a mushroom patch outdoors, or to inoculate a suitable mushroom food, such as a dead limb, that is grown indoors under controlled conditions. A mushroom farmer living near my home town of Greeneville, Tennessee, developed one of the world's first successful farms for truffles, the exorbitantly priced subterranean darlings of gourmet chefs worldwide. (Read more at www.tennesseetruffle.com.) You probably won't be able to duplicate his efforts. But anyone can grow field mushrooms, shiitakes, and a few others with minimal effort (and maximal luck). If you think mushroom farming might be for you, see the Appendix for additional information.

Pond Products

To produce ornamental or food fish you will need a pond larger than most suburban lots could accommodate, but even a twelve-by-twelve-foot pond can produce an abundant and continuous supply of aquatic plants. Garden ponds have become fashionable all across the country, and many garden centers cater to the trend. If there's a pond center in your area, check on the possibility of selling them water lilies or other aquatic plants. The productivity of most aquatic plant species is nothing short of amazing, and hundreds of

PHOTO BY JOHN TULLOCK

Even a small pond will produce abundant water lilies

varieties exist from which to glean possible product ideas. Of course, you should weigh the potential for sales against the investment of space, money, and labor that even a small pond entails. Expect to spend several hundred dollars just to get started, even if you do your own digging. Read up on ponds and pond keeping before you "dive into" such an extensive project.

Other Ideas

An extensive listing of alternative crops for small farmers has been compiled by the National Agricultural Library of the USDA. The list is available online at *www.nal.usda.gov/afsic/pubs/altlist.shtml.* Not all of these ideas are practical for a suburban microfarm, but a great many are.

chapter thirteen

Make a Selection of Successful Strategies

If you are ready to start harvesting profits from your backyard but remain unsure as to where to begin, here are some specific suggestions to get you started. None of these ideas is foolproof. Success will depend upon your ability to match the output of your microfarm to the needs and desires of your local market. However, similar strategies have worked for others. The information offered below is tailored to growing in Zone 6, where I live. If you live in another zone, you will need to modify your crop plan accordingly.

The Greens Machine

Lettuce and other fresh greens sell reliably at almost any farmers' market. Health advisors of every stripe seem to agree that leafy greens rank among the most nutritious foods, eating salad as part of a weight loss program has become a cliché, and so-called field greens now appear even on fast-food menus. Because no good way to preserve lettuce exists, it remains the one crop always eaten fresh. More importantly from the farmer's point of view, lettuces and other salad greens can be brought to market in as little as a month from sowing. Even though one of the biggest producers of organic salads processes more than 25 million servings per week, plenty of room exists in your market for salads that are quality-grown, dewy-fresh, and locally sourced.

Review the information on lettuce and other salad greens in Chapter 8 before devising your crop plan. Lettuce comes in so many cultivars that you can grow this species exclusively and still have plenty of variety in your offerings. Therefore, start your plan with lettuces. (Other greens can be added to your product mix if you have the space.) Because all the greens crops thrive on cool weather, use extending techniques at both ends of the growing season to give you the longest possible harvest time. About nine months of harvest is possible here in Zone 6, for example, if plants are grown under a polyethylene hoop house during late winter and again in autumn.

Divide your planting space into blocks that you will plant in sequence on a weekly basis. This is to insure an uninterrupted supply, once the harvest begins. Begin sowing seeds about a month before the frost date, earlier if you are using a season extender. Subdivide your planting block by variety, rather than mixing different ones in a single space.

Because each cultivar will react a little differently to the growing conditions you provide, keeping the various types separate allows you to pick only those that have properly matured. You can always mix them after harvest, if you prefer to sell that way.

Lettuce transplants in a raised bed

Under good conditions, looseleaf lettuce should yield about six ounces of salable product per square foot. At $5 per six-ounce bag (about three average servings) a forty-by-fifty-foot growing space (not counting access paths) will produce $10,000 in salads in a season.

The Salsa System

Here is an idea that capitalizes on the notion of offering vegetables that go together. Pick a recipe with which lots of people are likely to be familiar. Grow all the vegetables needed to prepare the recipe. Offer these vegetables in the correct proportions as a "package deal." Salsa, one of the most popular condiments, offers one option, but you could do this with other recipes, too. A "salsa basket" could contain two tomatoes, six scallions, two jalapeño peppers, and a small bunch of cilantro. Don't forget to include a recipe. Lime juice is the only other ingredient needed besides a little salt. You could even add a purchased lime to the basket, if your market rules permit this. Look over cookbooks to find other recipes, such as ratatouille, that are composed mostly of veggies.

The Instant Vegetable Garden

If you start your own vegetable plants, a practice I would encourage, you might want to try this idea to increase revenues. Take an ordinary ten-by-twenty nursery flat and fill it with enough vegetable plants to create a complete garden. You could seed lettuce into six-cell trays, beans into small peat pots, and tomatoes and peppers into larger peat pots. Stagger the seed sowing so you end up with, say, six cells of three-week-old lettuce plants and six more cells of one-week-old ones, to give the customer a longer harvest season. Do the same with early and late tomatoes. Sell the flats in mid-spring, when all these starts could go into the ground at about the same time. Write up a couple of pages of care instructions to include with each sale, and offer the entire flat for a single price.

The Instant Wildflower Garden

Fill a liner flat with three-inch pots of wildflowers that will grow well together, and offer the whole thing as a package. I suggest three to six plants each of three to five species. Good choices here in my part of the country would be three wood poppies, three bluebells, three foamflowers, and three cranesbill geraniums. All four species grow in rich, moist, well-drained soil in dappled shade, and between them cover both a spectrum of color (yellow, blue, white, and pink) and bloom times (wood poppy and bluebells early, foamflower midseason, geranium a bit later). The beauty of this idea is that by doing the planning for the customer, you overcome their reluctance to launch a new garden project and make their first season of effort nearly foolproof. Help see that it is by including an instructional flyer with every purchase. The end result will likely be a wildflower "convert" who will return to you for more.

Container Herb Gardens

This works the same in principle as the preceding idea. In effect, you are providing the customer a "crop plan" without their having to do the mental heavy lifting. Including edible flowers in a container along with herbs makes the whole thing more decorative and therefore more appealing. Applying the "spill, fill, and thrill" principle to a small container might lead you to use lemon thyme as the "spill" plant (two flavors for the price of one), extra curly parsley as the "fill," and gem marigold (edible blooms all season) for the "thrill."

A Succession of Edible Flowers

I love introducing people to edible flowers. One of the common refrains I hear is "How do you know which ones are okay to eat?" Don't just advise customers to search for the info on the Internet. Instead, say, "All you need to do is purchase one of my preplanted edible flower gardens." You can do this in a flat for transplanting or a mixed container, or both. A mixed container, for example, could contain three to five annual varieties, such as violas, gem marigolds, and nasturtiums, for a riot of color and a long season of blooms. Don't overlook the artistic possibilities, either. Nasturtiums and marigolds tend toward the warmer end of the spectrum, mostly reds, yellows, and oranges. The viola variety, therefore, will probably look best if it blooms in complementary yellow and gold tones. It will also be the earliest bloom, with the others to follow later in the season to carry the theme all summer.

Baby Vegetables

Baby vegetables are always popular with gourmet cooks, and typically are ready for market sooner than their full-size counterparts. You can market thinnings, for example, from spinach, carrots, and lettuces as baby crops, and later sell the fully mature crops, too. New potatoes are another classic example. Supplement these immature items with produce from cultivars that are naturally petite when fully developed, such cherry tomatoes and the berry-like currant tomato varieties. With a bit of searching, you can find cultivars of most common vegetables that will yield superb "babies."

Rent-to-Bloom

Orchid growers have been renting plants for years, and there is no reason why the technique won't work with other plant varieties. You apply your skills to growing specimen-quality container plants, then rent them out by the month or for a one-time event. Orchid growers sometimes offer a variation on this basic idea, wherein they provide plants in bloom during an agreed-upon time frame. Periodically, plants whose blooms have begun to fade are replaced with fresh ones. The faded specimens are brought back to the greenhouse, where they recuperate and are rented again when their blooms return. Check with caterers, wedding planners, and office maintenance companies for possible markets for rented plants.

Hardy Orchids

If you can be the first in your area to introduce gardeners to a new plant, you can capture a lot of sales before potential competitors realize it. This is what I was able to do with hardy orchids (those that will survive a winter outdoors in the temperate zone). My strategy consisted of producing a large number of *Bletilla striata*, a relatively easy-to-grow variety, and offering it exclusively to my best garden center customer. Fortunately for me, the *Bletilla* found a ready market, and I was able to expand sales the following year by including other hardy orchid varieties in my inventory.

Container Gardens

Depictions of life in miniature delight almost everyone. This probably accounts for the prevalence of bonsai trees on the benches of garden centers everywhere. True bonsai are trees that have been miniaturized through rigorous pruning and training. They often take years to create, and can sell for hundreds of dollars.

Because genuine bonsai lie far out of reach for people of ordinary means, I decided to experiment with "bonsai" gardens created from dwarf evergreen cultivars. These creations, which feature moss and other plants with tiny leaves in addition to the evergreens, have sold well, despite their comparatively high retail cost of $50 and up.

By careful arrangement of the plants and other elements, these container gardens can be made to fool the eye and please the aesthetic sense. I stick with designs that evoke the look of a Japanese print, but the possibilities for additional themes are limitless. I purchase the dwarf evergreens from specialty growers, but grow everything else myself. The moss, for example, grows near the condensate drain from my air conditioner. I start other plants from seed or cuttings. Ideal plants for this purpose will not only remain small in stature, they will also have leaves in proportion to their size and be relatively slow-growing. A look of antiquity can be achieved by encouraging the growth of moss on

PHOTO BY JOHN TULLOCK

A container garden

rocks, deadwood, or manmade objects that are subsequently included in your container garden designs.

Spreading the Wealth

Do not overlook the opportunities afforded by having a well-managed and productive garden spot, even if you do not have room to grow a whole lot of produce or cut flowers. Tough economic times are encouraging people to grow their own food like never before. During 2009, sales of vegetable seeds and plants were up dramatically at every retail outlet I consulted. Clearly, many people are growing food for the first time, or adding food crops to their existing gardens. Why not try to capitalize on this trend by teaching others to grow food? If you enjoy helping people and facilitating their learning, you can parlay your gardening expertise into income with little investment.

One approach to becoming a gardening instructor is to place a classified ad in your local weekly. Do this at least a month before the earliest planting date in your area. Potential students will want to get their gardens under way during the following spring.

Keep your fees reasonable. I suggest $50 per person for a course with two Saturday afternoon sessions. I would teach the basics of sustainable farming during the first session, and specifics for the top ten vegetables in your area for the second session. Keep the focus hands-on, and always be ready to modify your teaching style to meet the needs of your students. If you have a knack for "getting the message across" to a diverse audience, you may also find that demand exists for classes on other skills you have mastered, such as flower gardening.

If there is an institution in your area that offers adult education courses, you might be able to propose a course for inclusion in their catalog. This will typically require six months to a year of advance planning, and you should be prepared to submit a detailed outline of your proposed course, together with examples of supplementary materials, such as handouts. They will also want to see your resume. Working with an established institution provides credibility. The school will also have a better marketing and advertising program than you could muster. It is well worth the effort required to develop a course. Teaching others how to garden well can not only be a source of extra income, but also is deeply satisfying.

appendix

Help Is Out There

Books

Adams, Barbara Berst. *Micro Eco-Farming: Prospering from Backyard to Small Acreage in Partnership with the Earth.* (Auburn, CA: New World Publishing, 2005).

Aubrey, Sarah Beth. *Starting and Running Your Own Small Farm Business.* (North Adams, MA: Storey Publishing, 2008).

Avent, Tony. *So You Want to Start a Nursery?* (Portland, OR: Timber Press, 2003).

Bartholomew, Mel. *All New Square Foot Gardening.* (Franklin, TN: Cool Springs Press, 2005).

Coleman, Eliot. *Four Season Harvest: Organic Vegetables from Your Home Garden All Year Long.* 2nd edition, revised. (White River Junction, VT: Chelsea Green Publishing, 1999).

Coleman, Eliot. *The New Organic Grower: A Master's Manual of Tools and Techniques for the Home and Market Gardener.* (White River Junction, VT: Chelsea Green Publishing, 1995).

Creasy, Rosiland. *The Edible Flower Garden.* (Berkeley, CA: Periplus Editions, 2000).

Cullina, William. *Native Ferns, Mosses, and Grasses.* (Portland, OR: Timber Press, 2008).

Dirr, Michael. *Manual of Woody Landscape Plants: Their Identification, Ornamental Characteristics, Culture, Propagation and Uses.* 5th edition, revised. (Champaign, IL: Stipes Publishing, 1998).

Gibson, Eric. *Sell What You Sow: The Grower's Guide to Successful Produce Marketing.* (Auburn, CA: New World Publishing, 1994).

Gilman, Jeff. *The Truth about Organic Gardening*. (Portland, OR: Timber Press, 2008).

Harlan, Michael and Linda Harlan. *Growing Profits: How to Start and Operate a Backyard Nursery*. (Citrus Heights, CA: Moneta Publications, 2000).

Hirsch, David. *The Moosewood Restaurant Kitchen Garden*. (New York: Simon & Schuster, 1992).

Hoshizaki, Barbara Joe and Robbin Moran. *Fern Growers Manual: Revised and Expanded Edition*. (Portland, OR: Timber Press, 2001).

Lee, Andy W. and Patricia L. Foreman. *Backyard Market Gardening*. (Buena Vista, VA: Good Earth Publications, 1992).

Macher, Ron. *Making Your Small Farm Profitable*. (North Adams, MA: Storey Publishing, 1999).

Morse, Kitty. *Edible Flowers: A Kitchen Companion with Recipes*. (Berkeley, CA: Ten Speed Press, 1995).

National Audubon Society. *National Audubon Society Field Guide to North American Butterflies*. (New York: National Audubon Society, 1981).

Olsen, Sue. *Encyclopedia of Garden Ferns*. (Portland, OR: Timber Press, 2007).

Pollan, Michael. *In Defense of Food*. (New York: Penguin Press, 2008).

Pollan, Michael. *The Omnivore's Dilemma*. (New York: Penguin Press, 2006).

Schwenke, Karl. *Successful Small Scale Farming*. (Charlotte, VT: Garden Way Publishing, 1979).

Smith, Miranda. *Your Backyard Herb Garden*. (Emmaus, PA: Rodale Press, 1997).

Sturdivant, Lee. *Flowers for Sale: Growing and Marketing Cut Flowers: Backyard to Small Acreage*. (Friday Harbor, WA: San Juan Naturals, 1994).

Sturdivant, Lee. *Herbs for Sale: Growing and Marketing Herbs, Herbal Products and Herbal Know-How*. (Friday Harbor, WA: San Juan Naturals, 1994).

Sturdivant, Lee. *Profits from Your Backyard Herb Garden*. (Friday Harbor, WA: San Juan Naturals, 1995).

Taylor, T. M. *Secrets to a Successful Greenhouse Business: A Complete Guide to Starting and Operating a High-Profit Organic and Hydroponic Business That Benefits the Environment*. (Melbourne, FL: Green Earth Publishing, Inc., 2007).

Useful Websites

The following list is alphabetical by topic. The URLs were current as of December 20, 2008.

Alternative Crops

Information on all things *Stevia*-related can be found at *www .stevia.com*.

The many devotees of home poultry-keeping have spawned multiple websites, including *www.chickenkeeping.com, http://keepingchickens .blogspot.com, http://home.centurytel.net/thecitychicken*, and *http://home grownpoultry.com*.

Download a useful guide for beginning beekeepers from the University of Missouri at *http://extension.missouri.edu/explorepdf/agguides/pests/g07600.pdf.*

An interesting commercial beekeeping site with lots of links is found at *www.beeworks.com/index.html.*

Business Plans

Among the best sources for all kinds of information to help you build a business is the federal government's Small Business Administration. Extensive guides to business planning can be found at *www.sba.gov/smallbusinessplanner/index.html.*

Several nonprofit organizations offer help for small businesses. One of the most useful websites actually provides a free course in entrepreneurship. The section on business plans can be found at *www.myownbusiness.org/s2.* If you hope to expand your microfarm venture into a full-fledged home business, you might want to first read the essay posted by this organization's founder: *www.myown business.org/home_based_business.html.*

Butterfly Gardening

One of the best sites I've seen for butterfly information includes an interactive map allowing you to home in on the butterfly species found in any state: *www.thebutterflysite.com/gardening.shtml.*

Another website devoted to butterflies also has posted tons of information: *www.butterflywebsite.com/butterflygardening.cfm.*

The Missouri Botanical Garden has butterfly gardening information on its website at *www.butterflyhouse.org/butterflies/butterfly gardening.aspx.*

Many state-specific sites on butterflies and butterfly gardening exist. Search on "butterfly garden *state*" (replacing *state* with your state's name) to find them. Tennessee gardeners like me can begin with this publication, for example, which I found easily with the help of a search engine: *www.utextension.utk.edu/publications/pbfiles/PB1636.pdf.*

Butterfly field guides galore are advertised at this site: *www.butterflybuzz.com/page/290622.*

Color Wheels

For an artist's color wheel image, go to *www.colormatters.com/colortheory.html* or *www.artsconnected.org/toolkit/encyc_colorwheel.html.*

Community Supported Agriculture

The USDA has an Alternative Farming Systems Information Center with a wealth of resources concerning CSAs and other topics of interest to the suburban microfarmer. Check out the website at *www.nal.usda.gov/afsic/pubs/csa/csa.shtml.*

The University of Massachusetts at Amherst has an extensive web posting of CSA resources at *www.umassvegetable.org/food_farming_systems/csa.*

Another good resource portal for CSA is the Land Stewardship Project site: *www.landstewardshipproject.org/csa.html.*

Links to information on a broad range of topics of interest to the organic grower accompany the directory of CSAs at *www.greenpeople.org/csa.htm.*

For more specific information on CSA in your area, just search Google for "community supported agriculture *state*" (replacing *state* with your state's name).

Composting

Under the rubric of reducing the volume of the waste stream reaching America's landfills, the Environmental Protection Agency has posted an extensive collection of resources related to composting: *www.epa.gov/epawaste/conserve/rrr/composting/index.htm.*

Comprehensive composting information and resources can also be found at *www.howtocompost.org* and at *www.mastercomposter.com.*

Cover Cropping

Oregon State University has posted an excellent article on cover crops at *http://extension.oregonstate.edu/catalog/html/fs/fs304-e* including a table showing how much and when to sow for a small plot, along with other valuable data.

South Carolina's Clemson University publishes a data table of cover crops at *http://hgic.clemson.edu/factsheets/HGIC1252.htm.*

Cornell University offers a cover crop fact sheet at *www.gardening .cornell.edu/factsheets/ecogardening/impsoilcov.html.*

Cut Flowers

Virginia Tech University has posted an extremely useful table of cut flower crop information at *www.ext.vt.edu/pubs/envirohort/426 -619/426-619.html.*

Gardeners in the northern plains should check North Dakota State University's recommendations for cut flower crops at *www .ag.ndsu.edu/pubs/alt-ag/flowers.htm.*

Farmers' Market Locations

According to the Agricultural Marketing Service (AMS) of the U.S. Department of Agriculture, there are now over 4,500 farmers' markets in the United States. The AMS has a searchable database of them at *http://apps.ams.usda.gov/FarmersMarkets.*

Farmers' Market Dot Com not only has an index of markets by state and by cities within a state, the site also posts sources for apparel, gifts, and other items of interest to market growers. See *http://farmersmarket.com*.

More and more chefs are discovering the values of locally produced food. The Chef-2-Chef networking website posts a national farmers' market directory at *http://marketplace.chef2chef.net/farmer -markets*. Explore this site for wide-ranging information about professional chefs and their work.

Slow Food USA is part of an international grassroots movement to help people eat better, healthier, and, above all, locally. The organization has chapters across the country, and sponsors numerous events and activities of interest to the suburban farmer. Find the nearest chapter at *www.slowfoodusa.org/index.php/local_chapters*.

National Directory of Fruit Stands and Farmers' Markets posts a map of the United States with links to seasonal fruit vendors, as well as farmers' markets and the state agencies that oversee them, at *www.fruitstands.com*.

Farmers have been consulting the Old Farmer's Almanac for over two centuries. Not surprisingly, the publication returns the favor with a listing of farmers' markets at *www.almanac.com/garden/ farmersmarkets/states/index.php*. In addition, the website offers plenty of other garden information you will value, whether or not you grow for market.

Fern Growing

With more than a century of experience behind it, the American Fern Society is a great source of information about ferns. Membership puts you in touch with fern lovers the world over. See *http:// amerfernsoc.org*.

Find out who is growing ferns commercially from this specialty nursery listing: *www.nurseriesonline.us/specialistNurseries/Ferns.htm*.

Herbs, Edible Flowers, and Fruits

Ever the farmer's friend, the USDA has compiled a list of resources on medicinal herb marketing at *www.nal.usda.gov/afsic/AFSIC_pubs/mherb.htm*.

Marketing advice for the home herb grower is posted at *www.home-herb-garden.com/commgrow.html*.

The growing trade in nutraceuticals has spawned a website at *www.nutraceuticalsworld.com*.

Unsure as to the right market niche for your herb business? Read this informative article: *http://herbgardens.about.com/od/profitfrom herbs/a/herbplan.htm*.

The following site also covers herb markets, and much more: *www.everythingherb.com/herbmarket.html*.

The Herb Research Foundation is a membership site devoted to all things herbal: *www.herbs.org*.

A useful chart of edible and nonedible flowers is posted at *http://homecooking.about.com/library/weekly/blflowers.htm*.

ATTRA, the National Sustainable Agriculture Information Service (formerly called Appropriate Technology Transfer for Rural Areas), has information on both growing and marketing edible flowers in downloadable form: *http://attra.ncat.org/attra-pub/edible flowers.html*.

Check out this edible flower leaflet from North Carolina State University, which also contains a link to information on poisonous plants: *http://attra.ncat.org/attra-pub/edibleflowers.html*.

Entice your customers to cook with edible flowers. This site offers some suggestions for recipes: *www.starchefs.com/edible_flowers/html/index.shtml*.

Virginia Tech has posted a useful guide to small fruit growing in the home garden at *www.ext.vt.edu/pubs/envirohort/426-840/426 -840.html*.

This PDF file from Kansas State University provides a helpful table for planning your small fruit-growing space: *www.oznet.ksu .edu/library/hort2/mf352.pdf*.

Integrated Pest Management

The Resource Guide for Organic Insect and Disease Management, posted at *www.nysaes.cornell.edu/pp/resourceguide/index.php*, is a publication of the New York State Agricultural Extension Service and Cornell University. It covers a wide range of techniques and is highly recommended.

The United States Environmental Protection Agency has published an extensive IPM fact sheet at *www.epa.gov/pesticides/fact sheets/ipm.htm*.

A useful trap cropping table can be found at *www.oisat.org/ control_methods/cultural__practices/trap_cropping.html*.

An extensive image library that helps you diagnose crop diseases and deficiencies is published by the University of Massachusetts at Amherst: *www.umassvegetable.org/soil_crop_pest_mgt/disease_mgt/ index.html*.

Marketing

For a comprehensive look at many aspects of growing for market, check out this document from the USDA: *http://marketingout reach.usda.gov/info/99manual/99manual.htm*.

Free market analysis is available at *www.freedemographics.com*.

Search demographic information by state at *www.clrsearch .com/clrroadtrip?type=community*.

Mushrooms

The best place to begin your quest for mushroom growing and foraging information is the website of the Mycological Society of America: *http://msafungi.org*.

Another great site for the mushroom enthusiast is MykoWeb. Check out the article on getting started at *www.mykoweb.com/ articles/cultivation.html*.

Native Plants

A good introduction to native plant gardening, together with numerous links, has been posted by the U.S. Forest Service at *www .fs.fed.us/wildflowers/nativegardening/index.shtml*.

Search on "native plant society *state*" (replacing *state* with your state's name) to find the website of your local organization.

Orchids

The American Orchid Society website should be your first stop for information on orchids: *www.aos.org*.

An extensive posting of links to orchid suppliers, growers, and more can be found at *www.orchidmall.com*.

Organic Farming Methods

Find links galore at the website of the National Sustainable Agriculture Information Service (ATTRA): *http://attra.ncat.org*.

The Rodale Institute has been the leader in the U.S. organic farming movement; see *www.rodaleinstitute.org*.

Another in-depth site for organic methods is Sustainable Agriculture Research and Education (SARE): *www.sare.org*.

Organic vegetable growers will want to consult Sustainable Table at *www.sustainabletable.org*.

Also check the National Campaign for Sustainable Agriculture (NCSA): *www.sustainableagriculture.net/site/PageServer?pagename=NCSA_Home*.

Trellising

Fine Gardening magazine has a superbly illustrated article on tomato trellising and pruning on its website: *www.taunton.com/finegardening/how-to/articles/pruning-tomatoes.aspx?*.

Advice on trellising vegetables from the National Gardening Association can be found at *www.garden.org/foodguide/browse/veggie/vines_care/642*.

Vegetable Crop Information

Texas A&M University has published a set of production guides for vegetable crops, including typical yields, at *http://aggie-horticulture.tamu.edu/extension/vegetable/cropguides*.

Crop yields from small spaces can be found in "Planting a Home Vegetable Garden," published by Iowa State University. Download the PDF at *www.extension.iastate.edu/Publications/PM819.pdf*.

The Ag Center of Louisiana State University developed a crop yield table for home gardens in 2007: *www.lsuagcenter.com/en/lawn_garden/home_gardening/vegetables/cultural_information/Expected+Vegetable+Garden+Yields.htm*.

The USDA has posted a handbook for the storage of vegetables and other crops at *www.ba.ars.usda.gov/hb66*.

Search the extensive database of fruit and vegetable information, including storage methods, uses, and more at *www.fruitsandveggies morematters.org/?page_id=164*.

One of the most valuable sources of information for growers is your state's cooperative extension service. Find your local offices at *www.csrees.usda.gov/Extension*.

Vegetable Market Pricing
Market prices for vegetables across North America are compiled at *www.todaymarket.com*. You will need to purchase a subscription, but the site offers a one-week free trial.

Organic vegetable and livestock prices can be found at the USDA's Economic Research Service site: *www.ers.usda .gov/Data/OrganicPrices*.

Water Gardens
The University of Georgia has posted an excellent summary article on water gardening at *http://pubs.caes.uga.edu/caespubs/ horticulture/watergarden.htm*.

Download the water garden advice from the Southern Regional Aquaculture Center at *www.aquanic.org/publicat/usda_rac/efs/srac/ 435fs.pdf*.

Tables

VEGETABLE PLANTING GUIDE AND HARVEST TIMES			
Crop	Spacing*	Planting Depth	Days to Maturity
Bean	4 in.	2 in.	60
Beet	2 in.	½ in	50–70
Carrot	2 in.	½ in	90
Cucumber	36 in.	1 in.	60–90
Lettuce	4 in.	¼ in.	60–90
Melon	48 in.	1 in.	120
Okra	24 in.	½ in.	50–70
Pea	2 in.	2 in.	60
Radish	2 in.	½ in.	30
Scallion	1 in.	½ in.	90–120
Spinach	2 in.	1 in.	90
Squash	24 in.	1 in.	90–150
Turnip	4 in.	½ in.	45–50

*Spacing assumes growth in a raised bed, not rows.

VEGETABLE TRANSPLANTS SEEDING AND HARVEST TIMES			
Name	Spacing*	Days to Transplant	Days to Maturity
Broccoli	18 in.	60	90
Brussels sprouts	18 in.	60	120
Cabbage	12 in.	60	90
Cauliflower	18 in.	60	90–120
Eggplant	18 in.	60	90–120
Leek	12 in.	60	120–150+
Lettuce	6 in.	14–21	60
Pepper	18 in.	60	90–120
Tomato	18 in.	60	90–120

*Spacing assumes growth in a raised bed, not rows.

POTS FILLED FROM A 3.8 CUBIC FOOT BALE OF GROWING MIX		
Size	Number	Cost/Plant*
4 in. sq.	398	.06
4½ in. sq.	350	.07
6 in. round	102	.245
8 in. round	47	.53
48 cell flat	43	.012
72 cell flat	49	.007

*Based on $25 per bale of mix

NURSERY CONTAINERS PER 100 SQUARE FEET		
Type	Dimensions (in.)	Number
Flat	11 × 21.5	48
Liner tray	18 × 18	60
#1 pot	6 (dia.)	400
#2 pot	8.5 (dia.)	200
#5 pot	12 (dia.)	100
#15 pot	16 (dia.)	56

Index